THE Cure FOR THE "Perfect" Life

KATHI LIPP
CHERI GREGORY

HARVEST HOUSE PUBLISHERS
EUGENE, OREGON

Cover design by Harvest House Publishers, Inc., Eugene, Oregon

Cover photo © Harvest House Publishers

Published in association with the Books & Such Management, 52 Mission Circle, Suite 122, PMB 170, Santa Rosa, CA 95409-5370, www.booksandsuch.com.

THE CURE FOR THE "PERFECT" LIFE
Copyright © 2014 by Kathi Lipp and Cheri Gregory
Published by Harvest House Publishers
Eugene, Oregon 97402
www.harvesthousepublishers.com

Library of Congress Cataloging-in-Publication Data
   The cure for the perfect life / Cheri Gregory and Kathi Lipp.
     pages cm
   ISBN 978-0-7369-5700-7 (pbk.)
   ISBN 978-0-7369-5701-4 (eBook)
   1. Christian women—Religious life. 2. Success—Religious aspects—Christianity. 3. Self-actualization (Psychology)—Religious aspects—Christianity I. Gregory, Cheri, editor of compilation.
   BV4527.C845 2014
   248.8'43—dc23

                            2014002584

Contents

How the "Perfect" Life Snuck Up on Us

✳

No one would ever label me (Kathi) a perfectionist.

- You can't eat off my floor. Well, you could, but I wouldn't suggest it.
- My husband would say that our house is cluttered enough to be comfy.
- I can fall asleep with a basket full of unfolded laundry in the next room.
- No part of me admires Martha Stewart.

Typical thoughts of perfection

However, as many of you know, perfectionism comes in disguised and sneaky forms.

- I've spent a lifetime caring what complete strangers think about me.
- I have to fight thoughts of unworthiness every single day.
- I have a hard time believing that I should be allowed to enjoy anything in my life—everyone else is so much more deserving than I am.

I also have this constant feeling that everyone else "gets it" (whatever "it" is—marriage, parenting, work, friendships, God) and I don't. It is a struggle every single day of my life, feeling like I'm out of the loop—that everyone else was handed some manual to life.

And while I may not look like the classic perfectionist, the hurts that come from my behavior when I'm living by the beliefs of the bully of perfectionism are just as destructive:

- I will pick up the check in almost every situation because I feel that I've taken up the other person's time.

- I will run out the night before an event and spend too much on clothes so that I appear to fit in.

- I spend ten times more time worrying about how other people feel in situations than being concerned about my own health in these relationships.

It's a fine line I walk. I want to put others' needs ahead of my own. I'm the drowning woman who is throwing life preservers to people on the lifeboat so they will have something to rest their heads on in their deck chairs.

Perfectionism isn't Christian. It's just crazy.

And I (Cheri) would never have labeled myself a perfectionist. When I was a teenager, my poor mother—who kept an immaculate house, complete with white sofas and carpets—often told me, "Just looking in your room I *feel* messy!"

Shortly after I got married, my mom came to visit. She took one look at the sad state of my housekeeping and told my husband, "I'm so sorry. You have no idea how hard I tried."

I never saw myself as a perfectionist because I couldn't keep a spotless home as my mother did. But it turns out that trying hard was something my mom and I had in common. We just tried hard at different things.

The "just try harder" mantra made me

- a student who argues for the extra point when she gets 99 percent and who cries if her A has a minus.

- a teacher who skips family gatherings because she can't face her students until her lesson plans are just right.

- a wife who tries to overhaul her husband so that she can finally have a happy marriage.

- a parent who explains the latest unforeseen circumstances to her children's teachers. Dozens of times. Even when they're in college.

I tried as hard as I could but still failed (which I defined as getting a lower grade than I wanted, hearing criticism of any kind, being publically humiliated, feeling foolish...you get the idea).

So I started following a secret second mantra: "Don't bother trying." Playing it safe turned me into

- an employee who doesn't speak up during staff meeting so her input can't get shot down.

- a woman who automatically thinks, *She's not going to like me* when introduced to someone for the first time.

- a friend who lets a call from a BFF in crisis go to voice mail because she feels too inadequate to answer.

- a pastor's wife who skips church because her own family drama has left her too drained to put on her game face for the day.

- a daughter who doesn't visit home very often because she can't fix her mother's Alzheimer's disease.

I've exhausted myself trying hard when it really didn't matter. And I've not tried at all when it actually did.

Which are the major symptoms of Try-Harder Living (THL)...with or without white carpet.

Even though we have different life stories, we've both succumbed to Try-Harder Living. We used to look for the nice, polite ways to follow God's call. We caved to others' expectations for too long. We finally decided to stop taking our cues from the world and start asking ourselves, "What does God want from me...and have *for* me?"

And we've come to the conclusion: there is no nice, polite way to do this. There's no easy way to leave the life that's been expected of us and to start living the brave, not so neatly tied up life that God is calling us to.

We have to rebel. We have to make choices that are countercultural to our society, our families of origin, and even our churches.

We're guessing that as you've read our stories you've said, "Me too!" at one point or another (or perhaps several points). Most women we know are fighting THL to some degree.

We get it. We've been there. We have the souvenir travel mugs. And because life isn't perfect, those mugs have leaked all over our shirts. (It's the official uniform for the recovering perfectionist—a nice white shirt with a huge stain down the front.)

Come join our rebellion. We have cupcakes. The frosting is a little mushed, but hey, they still taste great. And they aren't homemade. But we're okay with that.

As we share our own rebel stories and strategies, we hope you will

- exchange outdated views of who you "should be" for a clear vision of who you are in Christ.

- take control of that too long to-do list so it no longer controls you.

- stop striving to maintain an image and live with more freedom day-to-day.

- overcome the tyranny of "more" and live radically with the abundance of "enough."

- stop trying to earn others' approval and learn to rest in God's lavish unconditional love.

Before jumping in, we want to take you on a quick big-picture tour of this book. In Part 1, you'll meet the four bullies of Try-Harder Living: Perfectionism, People-Pleasing, Performancism, and Procrastination. (Don't worry, we'll introduce you to them from a safe distance!) You'll get familiar with what each one is and isn't, learn its signature weapon, watch it in action, and see how it can infiltrate different areas of your life.

In Part 2, you'll discover the main force of Try-Harder Living and the core choice of Braver Living. Together, we'll walk through the first key steps toward Braver Living. And you'll receive valuable information about your unique rebel strengths, plus a few words of warning, before charging into battle.

In Part 3, you'll explore twelve of the most common bully beliefs of Try-Harder Living. Early in each chapter, you'll take a self-assessment to help you discover how much that particular belief is trapping you in your pursuit of the "perfect" life. You'll discover vital truths from God's Word to combat these bully beliefs. We'll share strategies that have worked for us in making the switch from Try-Harder Living to Braver Living, and help you envision yourself making this same shift.

If you're a writing kind of gal, grab yourself a journal. Jot down your self-assessment scores, your reflections on your answers, and what you're learning about yourself as you keep reading. If you're a blogger, blogging your way through these twelve chapters would make a fabulous series to share with your readers.

One more thing: grab a friend. Neither of us could have walked our journey or written this book alone. We needed each other. Ecclesiastes 4:9-10 tells why:

> Two are better than one,
>   because they have a good return for their labor:
> If either of them falls down,
>   one can help the other up.
> But pity anyone who falls
>   and has no one to help them up.

So find yourself a buddy who's ready to learn how to Live Braver too. And come join us at rebel headquarters: https://www.facebook.com/TinyActsOfRebellion. We're all in this journey together!

PART 1

Why Trying Harder Only Makes Things Worse

✳

If you suspect that you, too, suffer from an undiagnosed case of Try-Harder Living, you may be wondering

- *How do I know if it's time for me to rebel?*
- *If so, exactly what do I rebel against?*
- *How do I become a rebel?*

We'll answer all of these questions and more. But first, a quick diagnostic test. Write in the blank for each statement the number that best reflects the extent to which you agree or disagree with that statement.

Strongly Disagree = 5 Disagree = 4 Neutral = 3 Agree = 2 Strongly Agree = 1

1. ___ I'm flexible about how things get done: my way, your way, either way.

2. ___ I am willing to try, fail, and learn from my mistakes.

3. ___ I allow myself to feel big emotions, from anger to sorrow to joy.

4. ___ I know how to appropriately process and express negative emotions.

5. ___ I have plenty of chances for fun, recreation, and celebration each month.

6. ___ I regularly get seven or more hours of sleep per night.

7. ___ I take responsibility for my own feelings and reactions; I expect other people to take responsibility for theirs.

8. ___ I am secure in my identity as a child of God; while I love my family, friends, work, and hobbies, none of them define me.

9. ___ I make a point to keep my home, calendar, and life uncluttered.

10. ___ I am intentional about budgeting and balancing both my time and energy.

11. ___ I ask for help as soon as I need it.

12. ___ I am comfortable declining invitations and requests; I communicate pleasantly and confidently when doing so.

_____ TOTAL SCORE

The ideal range on the Try-Harder Living test is 12–24. (We're guessing that if you're reading this book by choice, your score is higher than ideal!)

(handwritten margin note: where did you fit.)

25–36 = mild THL
37–48 = full-blown THL
49–60 = severe THL

How do you know if it's time to rebel? If you've got Try-Harder Living to any degree, the sooner the better! THL worsens exponentially when left untreated. If you're just at the mild stage, praise God and rebel while it's still an easy choice.

The longer you wait, the harder it gets, because the four troublemakers that cause THL are parasites. They are hell-bent on dominating your life. Their goal is to destroy any sense of self you have left.

Meet the Gang

Try-Harder Living has four main instigators: Perfectionism, People-Pleasing, Performancism, and Procrastination. These bullies work together. When you're fighting with one, the other three cheer him on and jump in as needed.

Although each bully has his own special weapon, they all share one common goal: to convince you to pour all your energy into creating and maintaining an image. This image is based on who they say you *should* be. Their criteria, of course, change from day to day. This keeps you dancing to their demands, right on the edge of burnout.

To break free from these bullies, we need to know a bit about them. Forewarned is forearmed, after all. So in the next four chapters you'll discover how to identify each one. And you'll learn to recognize the strategies they use against you as they aim to paralyze you with Try-Harder Living.

CHAPTER 1

Perfectionism

"I'm always trying harder to look good enough."

✳

A quick question to ask yourself if you suspect you're getting hammered by Perfectionism is *Am I obsessed with getting certain results?* If your answer is yes, Perfectionism is the likely culprit. If you listen closely, you can hear him yelling, "That's not good enough! Try harder!"

Perfectionism Defined

When we asked our blog readers and Facebook friends to tell us what they thought about Perfectionism, one woman said, "If 'perfectionism' means striving for a higher standard than mediocrity, then I don't think it's a problem!" Another suggested, "I think the current generation of young women could use a good dose of 'perfectionism.' Too many of them are like 'whatever' about everything!"

Let's agree right up front that when we use the term Perfectionism, we are *not* referring to

- conscientiousness
- becoming more like Christ
- a commitment to excellence

In her devotional *Prayers for a Woman's Soul,* Julie Gilles separates excellence from Perfectionism:

> Lofty standards and a desire to always get it right may seem like noble goals, but they only set us up for intense pressure, frustration, and disappointment. It's not that we shouldn't strive for excellence, but we need to understand

the difference between pursuing excellence and pursuing perfection. True excellence is simply doing our very best— perfectionism demands a flawless performance at all times.[1]

Bill Gaultiere of *Soul Shepherding* calls Perfectionism "a manifestation of anxiety, straining to be ideal or to have an ideal experience of some kind. The perfectionists of the Bible are the Pharisees. Perfectionism goes with legalism, pride, and judgmentalism."[2]

For our purposes, we're going to borrow Brené Brown's definition of Perfectionism: "Perfectionism is a self-destructive and addictive belief system that fuels this primary thought: 'If I look perfect, and do everything perfectly, I can avoid or minimize the painful feelings of shame, judgment, and blame.'"[3]

Perfectionism is characterized by relentless criticism of self and others.

Perfectionism in Action

Two decades ago, while taking a graduate literature course, I (Cheri) signed up to give an in-class presentation and bring snacks on the same day. You might think I was simply being efficient, but the truth is I was being driven by Perfectionism. I'd given birth to my son only a couple of months earlier. Our lives had been a hodgepodge of NICU visits, car trouble, nursing issues, and sleeplessness ever since.

In addition to preparing my twenty-minute presentation for class, I decided to make snacks that matched my topic: the symbolism of the hand-shaped birthmark in one of Nathaniel Hawthorne's short stories. I made three different types of tea sandwiches, all cut with a hand-shaped cookie cutter.

But that still wasn't enough. The week before my presentation, I spent every spare moment sewing myself a new dress and jacket to wear to class. (The jacket had piping trim. If you sew, you know I was insane. If you don't sew, trust me: I was insane.)

The sandwiches did look amazing. Everyone burst out with exclamations of, "No way!" and "Wow!" when I unveiled them. And my outfit was stunning. My professor kept gushing about it, especially when I casually let slip that I'd "sewn it myself last week."

Right about now you may be wondering, "And this was bad because...?"

<u>Yes, this was bad. Very bad. Because I did none of this out of love. I felt no joy.</u> I sewed every stitch and cut every bread slice because I felt like I, on my own, was completely inadequate. My trying harder and even harder and still harder was motivated by my desperation for my presentation to be "good enough."

I was on the verge of exhaustion during those months. Yet, I devoted hours to sewing a new outfit and making fancy sandwiches—hours I could have invested in catching up on sleep, enjoying my husband, being present for my children.

Instead, I robbed us all of my time, energy, and availability. For what great purpose? To complete two unnecessary projects above-and-beyond. Two projects that ultimately did not matter. In fact, they were counterproductive. I ended up alienating myself from my classmates because they found me intimidating. In my efforts to impress, I unknowingly set the bar so high, nobody felt they could come close—to my achievements or to me.

That dress and those sandwiches are long gone. But my memory of fatigue and desperation during Jonathon's first year still lingers. As does my recall of how lonely I was; nobody would come close, and I couldn't figure out why.

Contrast my striving with the skilled workmanship of a craftsman we met last summer. In celebration of our twenty-fifth wedding anniversary, Daniel and I spent a week in Ashland, Oregon, at a beautiful little studio called the Art-Y Cottage. It was filled with the most exquisite woodwork either of us has ever seen. Every corner was a precise 90-degree angle. The drawers and cabinet doors were in perfect alignment; they opened and closed with absolute precision.

We spent an hour in Tom Saydah's workshop, keenly aware that we were in the presence of a skilled workman who loved his craft. His various workspaces were thoughtfully laid out. As we walked through, he picked up pieces of wood, caressing them affectionately. He handed them to us as if he were showing off his babies. Tom told us the type of wood, where he'd purchased it, and his plans for it.

Yes, he was "a perfectionist," but he was not driven by the bully of Perfectionism.

Everything in his workshop was intentionally set up in service of his gift, his offering, his skill. We sensed no fear in the air, no frantic need for our approval. He didn't do great work *so that* he would be a skilled craftsman—he did great work *because* he was a skilled craftsman.

How Others Perceive Perfectionism

Of the three hundred women who responded to our "Women Trying to Measure Up" survey, 70 percent considered themselves perfectionistic toward others, themselves, or both. As I read through their comments, I kept thinking, *How did she get inside my brain?*

Which of these sound familiar to you?

Perfectionism in Marriage

> "It's hard for me to go with the flow. And I know that drives my husband crazy."

> "I feel perpetual disappointment and discontent with the things my husband does for the family because I feel they aren't done right. I try very hard not to nag or demean his actions, but even when I succeed in keeping quiet, those thoughts are still there, bubbling under the surface."

Perfectionism in Parenting

> "I carried my perfectionistic upbringing over to my own children and would spend hours yelling at my four- and five-year-olds, 'HOW HARD IS IT TO PUT YOUR HOT WHEEL CARS IN THE BUCKET LABELED HOT WHEELS, LEGOS IN THE LEGO BUCKET, ARMY MEN IN THE ARMY BUCKET!' I am so embarrassed about that now. I missed so much of my kids being little because I was trying to live up to the perfectionistic standards that were ingrained in me."

Perfectionism in Relationships

> "I have to be the person to do everything right, without help from others. I can't show that I'm weak in aspects of my life

that others might see. For example; when my father passed away, I had to organize the funeral and help my mother and sister cope, as well as be strong for my children. I felt that if they saw me cry, they would perceive me as being weak and a failure. As a result of living my life this way, I think people see me as detached and unfriendly."

Perfectionism at Home

"I insist on a perfect house with a perfect yard. I end up being not just disappointed but angry because, after all, I'm doing it for them!"

Perfectionism at Work

"I see Perfectionism a lot at work. One person takes over and orders everyone else around because she feels that she is the only one who can do it right. We are supposed to be a team, but these people don't work well as part of a team. As a result, there are a lot of hurt feelings, a lot of bitterness, and people become more reluctant to work together to accomplish things."

Perfectionism with Self

"I expect that every project I begin, every conversation, every opportunity, must be just right and achieve all possible potential. It's exhausting, and the demands I put on myself cause me to be disappointed most of the time."

"I find myself wanting to do things right and overachieving at least partly for the wrong motives: wanting people to notice and think well of me. I'm looking for validation and feelings of worth."

"It was how I made sense of being sexually assaulted as a child—if I behaved better, then I wouldn't get hurt. So I worked hard at getting straight As, a great job that eventually led to a very senior position in a global public company. But

it was exhausting. And I still got hurt. However, the world
does reward perfectionism. Even if you don't get to perfect,
you are an overachiever and companies like overachievers."

It's so easy to wear our Perfectionist badges with pride, forgetting the
dangers of getting all buddy-buddy with this bully. But Perfectionism
is patient and sly. He'll wait until you're giving your best effort and then
shove you over the line to obsessing about results.

Comedian Ken Davis offers this caution: "A perfectionist is not
someone who is perfect; it is someone who is miserable, because they
can't get it right."[4] Know all too well what that kind of misery feels like?
We do too. And we want you to know how good it feels to send this
bully packing.

CHAPTER 2

People-Pleasing

"I'm always trying harder to seem nice enough."

✳

Am I obsessed with getting specific reactions? is the question that will help you catch People-Pleasing meddling in your affairs. This bully assures you that he has your best interests at heart and is just trying to help. "They don't look happy yet. Try harder!" is his motivational mantra.

People-Pleasing Defined

People-Pleasing is not the same thing as love; in fact, in many cases it is a major cause of the erosion of love. Nor is People-Pleasing the same thing as care, compassion, sympathy, or empathy. People-Pleasing involves

- putting the wants of others above one's own needs
- avoiding conflict
- basing self-worth on others' reactions
- feeling trapped, often to the point of martyrdom, by others' needs
- and keeping silent about one's own needs, wants, and opinions

In *What Happens When Women Say Yes to God*, Lysa TerKeurst spells out three reasons we people-please:

Fearful motives: "They might not like me if I say no."

Skewed intentions: "If I do this for them, will they be more likely to do that for me?"

19

Unrealistic expectations: "I just know if I give a little more, they'll affirm me. And I'm desperate for their attention."[5]

The consequences of People-Pleasing are often as overlooked as they are devastating. Georgia Shaffer, author of *Taking Out Your Emotional Trash*, cautions that "needing to keep or gain the approval of the people in our lives assaults us and wears us down. We have little time and energy left to do the things God calls us to do."[6]

Over time, People-Pleasing can morph into what Deborah Smith Pegues calls "the martyr attitude":

> Meet the false martyr. She sacrifices out of a false sense of obligation and derives satisfaction and self-esteem from the sympathy and attention it brings her from others…
>
> A martyr attitude can have a profoundly negative effect on relationships. Others usually find the false martyr exhausting and unpleasant to be around, primarily because false martyrs complain about their service. Further, some martyrs attempt to place a guilt trip on people who do not emulate or appreciate their sacrifices. Most people will resent being manipulated in this manner.[7]

People-Pleasing in Action

As I (Cheri) read our initial survey results, I was in for a surprise. I had expected the women to identify Perfectionism as the greatest evil known to womankind. But when I started reading the comments about People-Pleasing, I was shocked. Although the women gave Perfectionism a beating, their criticism of People-Pleasing was scathing. To my dismay, two words kept showing up as the ultimate results of People-Pleasing: *resentment* and *bitterness*. *I'm resentful and bitter*, I thought to myself, *but I'm a Perfectionist, not a People-Pleaser. How can this be?*

Eventually, I had to face the truth: I was a Perfectionist *and* a People-Pleaser.

I've come to recognize that People-Pleasing is my primary bully, with Perfectionism serving as his ever-present sidekick. Unbeknownst to me—but obvious to those close to me, especially my children—I have a highly developed martyr attitude.

Oh the times I've gone out of my way to do one of my children a favor! Of course, I've rarely told them how much of an inconvenience it was. No. I swore I would never be an "after all I've done for you…" kind of mother who burdened her children with guilt. I just wanted to be a loving mom who did nice things for her children.

Until I did nice things for them, and they failed to react with smiles of gratitude, that is. Or, worse yet, acted grumpy or upset, which was decidedly not in my plan. I wanted to do nice things for my children so they would be happy; at least that's the story People-Pleasing told me.

But with People-Pleasing running the show, it was impossible to tell truth from fiction. It's taken me years to realize that I didn't care so much if my kids were happy. I did nice things for them mainly because I could not tolerate them being upset. I needed them to at least seem okay so I could feel okay. When they weren't happy, I didn't want what was actually best for them. I wanted, and did, whatever would cause my own upset, triggered by their upset, to abate.

Thus, all the favors I did them. Thus, my resentment and bitterness. Thus, both my children floundering after they left home. All my niceness actually set them up for failure to launch.

I truly did not think of myself as a helicopter parent or smother mother or stalker mom during their high school years. But I was all of these. I jumped in to help too quickly. I didn't let them fall flat on their faces. I didn't let them pick themselves up, dust themselves off, and figure out what had happened let alone how to prevent it in the future. Instead, I meddled. I always cushioned the fall.

My reasons were understandable: I had experienced *inappropriate* pain and disappointment as a child and a teenager, so I was determined to keep my children from suffering as I had. But in protecting them from the *in*appropriate pain and disappointment, I went overboard and tried to protect them from *all* pain and disappointment.

While my kids were in high school, I thought that my involvement would produce wonderfully high GPAs that would snag scholarships that would launch strong college careers.

I was wrong.

Both kids snagged scholarships worth thousands of dollars but lost them all during their first year. Neither lasted in the Honors Program.

Why? I'd created the nice illusion that all they had to do was show up, be their wonderful selves, and everything else would just happen. Annemarie went into a major depression her freshman year when she discovered that, on her own, she didn't know how to keep clean laundry in her drawers, stay on top of homework, keep the GPA to maintain her scholarships, and remain in Honors. Jonathon, already an introvert, retreated into gaming for similar reasons.

I now wish they'd spent their final two years of high school as dorm students at the Christian boarding academy where I teach, instead of living at home. Getting away from me would have fostered greater independence. They would have learned many life skills and gained the maturity that comes from not having their own way all the time.

Yes, I would have missed them. But my job wasn't to hold on to them as long as possible or keep them as comfortable as I could. My job was to facilitate their maturity and autonomy. Had I focused on that long-range goal, they would have been spared unnecessary pain and struggle their freshmen and sophomore years of college.

But People-Pleasing never let me think beyond the present. People-Pleasing kept me hyper-vigilantly alleviating the immediate discomfort of each moment. So when they struggled during their freshman year of college, I blamed them for wasting our money. Because, of course, after all I'd done for them...

How Others Perceive People-Pleasing

Of the three hundred women who responded to our "Women Trying to Measure Up" survey, four out of every five considered themselves people-pleasers. As I read through the comments, I saw People-Pleasing—which I'd always dismissed as a harmless personality quirk—in the glaring light of harsh reality.

Which of these make you think, "Well, when you say it *that* way..."?

People-Pleasing in Marriage

> "The consequence of people-pleasing is that I get mad at my husband, and then there goes another weekend that we didn't get to do anything fun together. It keeps us from being close."

"My husband has felt neglected because I was more concerned with taking care of 'everyone else' than being with him."

"My husband gets frustrated with me because I'll fixate forever on one negative comment."

People-Pleasing in Parenting

"I've spent so much time making sure that my kids like me, I've had to fight hard in these later years to earn their respect. I've actually crippled my kids in some areas of their lives with my 'kindness.'"

"As a child, I was constantly seeking to earn my father's love and avoid his criticism. I tried to be always obedient so he would say something nice about me or to me."

People-Pleasing in Relationships

"I have to wear a mask all the time because I'm afraid people will reject the real me. It leaves me lonely."

"I have this huge sense of guilt when my friends feel shortchanged or when I have to tell one group of friends no in favor of another. I don't ever want my friends to be mad at me or to feel like I don't love them."

"I feel pulled in too many directions and can't please everyone at once."

People-Pleasing at Home

"I definitely take after my mom in this area. We both try so hard to please others that we sometimes tick them off instead. Making a decision is difficult because we would rather have people around us happy with their decisions than push our own, but others just want us to have an opinion!"

"I tend to say yes to everything, even when I don't want to. I end up with too much on my plate and don't have enough time to do things my family needs. My home is often neglected and left a mess."

People-Pleasing at Work

> "When you work for someone who is a people-pleaser, there's little confidence in knowing that decisions are firm. Instead, a people-pleaser might change the plan at any moment and without communicating the change, because they are driven to be liked by whoever they're with at the moment."

> "As a former kindergarten teacher, I might have forty-six positive parent-teacher conferences. But if one parent came in upset, that's all I could concentrate on."

People-Pleasing and Self

> "I am a 'words of affirmation' person, so I do find myself doing things to please people just to get that recognition. It can become a selfish act disguised as a selfless one."

> "I get hurt a lot because others don't care about me the way I care about them."

> "I fear folks rather than God."

> "There's a huge difference between being selfless and people-pleasing."

> "I now see people-pleasing as being a savior to everyone and replacing God with myself."

> "People-pleasing breaks the compass of your soul."

Trying hard to make people happy sure seems like the loving choice. The People-Pleasing bully assures you that it's not just the loving choice, it's the *Christian* choice. But he's no help when your hyper-vigilance over people's reactions makes you feel bitter and resentful. In fact, when you fall into martyr mode, expect him to turn on you.

Dealing with People-Pleasing is always a "heads I win, tails you lose" game: first he urges you to try harder to be nicer, and then he blames you for being too nice. We want to help you escape his self-defeating trap and enjoy the freedoms of living braver.

CHAPTER 3

Performancism

"I'm always trying harder to be seen doing enough."

✳

If you ask yourself, *Am I focusing so much on this project that I'm neglecting key people in my life?* and get the response, "Don't worry about them; they'll be fine," then you're being bossed by Performancism. He'll also insist, "Keep working. There's lots more to do."

Performancism Defined

Performancism is not the same thing as a strong work ethic. Nor is it practicing a skill to mastery. Just as workaholism is not merely working hard but an actual addiction to work, Performancism is a compulsive, insatiable craving for achievement.

In *Me, Myself, and Bob*, Phil Vischer of VeggieTales fame explores his own battles with Performancism:

> I had grown up drinking a dangerous cocktail—a mix of the gospel, the Protestant work ethic, and the American dream. My eternal value was rooted in what I could accomplish. My role here on earth was to dream up amazing things to do for God. If my dreams were selfless, God would make them all come true. My impact would be huge. The world would change. Children would rise up and call me blessed, and I would receive a hero's welcome into heaven. The most important thing, though, was to be busy. Industrious. Hardworking. A self-made man—er, Christian. The Savior I was following seemed, in hindsight, equal parts Jesus, Ben Franklin, and Henry Ford.[8]

Mary DeMuth, in her book *Beautiful Battle*, shares her own struggle:

> Oswald Chambers reminds me of the settled life God wants.
> He writes, "It is much easier to do something than to trust in
> God; we see the activity and mistake panic for inspiration."
> I've been living in that place of panic for several months. I've
> taken panic into myself, digested it, then produced more
> work and to-do lists than anyone could finish. Has that fre-
> netic activity helped me rise above my stress? No. Instead,
> trapped in myself and my worry, I've settled into Satan's lies,
> let stress have its way.[9]

And researcher Brené Brown condemns Performancism without
reservation:

> One of the most universal numbing strategies is what I call
> crazy-busy. I often say that when they start having twelve-
> step meetings for busy-aholics, they'll need to rent out foot-
> ball stadiums. We are a culture of people who've bought into
> the idea that if we stay busy enough, the truth of our lives
> won't catch up with us.[10]

Performancism in Action

"Whatever your hand finds to do, do it with all your might, for in
the realm of the dead, where you are going, there is neither working nor
planning nor knowledge nor wisdom" (Ecclesiastes 9:10).

"Whatever your hand finds to do" is a dangerous phrase for many of
us. Even before the influx of social media, we could find dozens of things
for our hands to do. How many times have we walked into Michaels
for a bottle of tacky glue and come out with bags of brand new hobbies? Enter Pinterest, and suddenly we have millions of "whatevers" our
hands can find to do!

But wait. Notice that two-letter word *it*?

This verse does not say, "Everything your hands happen to find to
do, do them all with all your might." That little *it* suggests that your
hands will find one thing to do at a time. And when you're doing that

one thing, you'll give it your all: your focus, your energy, your skills, your best efforts.

Ecclesiastes 9:10 is not an edict to find more to do. This verse is an *anti*-multitasking message. It recognizes that efficiency is often the enemy of effectiveness. Multitasking may work for some tasks. But multitasking kills relationships. Relationships require focus. Relationships require that the other person be your "one thing."

I (Cheri) would love to say that I've practiced doing one thing with all my might for decades. But it wasn't until my daughter broke her arm that I saw how much Performancism was dominating my life.

Annemarie fell while roller blading one night and then complained that her wrist hurt. I was on a tight schedule that week, with dozens of tasks that only I could do and several appointments only I could meet. I also had two all-day events several hours from home, and I was counting on sales from these events to help me earn an incentive trip.

"Ice it," I told her. "It's probably just sprained." I didn't know whether it was just sprained or not. My to-do list had no room for "take daughter to ER" until the weekend.

Two days later, Annemarie's wrist was still hurting badly. So I asked my parents, who lived an hour away, if they could take her in for an X-ray. I felt like a total heel when I got home that night to find Annemarie's arm in a cast and hear her declare, "It wasn't just broken in one place but two!"

Ten years later, I still regret that I chose tasks and productivity over my own daughter. I was so caught up in efficiency mode that I neglected one of the most important relationships in my life. Annemarie felt invalidated, since I'd spent several days telling her that she had "just a sprain." And she felt devalued, since all my important busyness took precedent over her health needs.

Not only does Performancism cause us to neglect important relationships with people, but it distorts our most important relationship: with God. "When we 'perform' for God, we expect Him to 'perform' for us. When He doesn't perform per our expectations, we feel unloved," says author and speaker Donna Jones.[11]

Performancism tells us that performance will result in love.

<u>That's backward.</u>

<u>Love always leads us</u> to take action. But performance, on its own, can't produce love.

We can "fake it 'til you make it" with some things in life, but not love. At some point, we'll be forced to recognize that we've not made it and that everything we have to show for our lifetime of efforts is fake.

How Others Perceive Performancism

Of the three hundred women who responded to our "Women Trying to Measure Up" survey, two-thirds considered themselves performancists. Many expressed pain and regret that <u>"doing" has too often taken priority over "being"</u> in their relationships.

Which of these hit home for you?

Performancism in Marriage

"I rob myself, my husband, and my children to be there for others and to work, work, work."

"On our last vacation, my husband was enjoying meandering. I had to mentally adjust my inner itinerary to say 'meander' before I could join him."

Performancism in Parenting

"I see so many parents pushing children to achieve academically to the point that it consumes their time and energy and dominates the relationship."

"Children end up feeling as if they are only valued for what they do instead of for who they are."

"My mother signed me up for every kind of lesson I could take in our hometown. She pushed me to excel in school and accepted nothing less than As. Now that I'm a teacher, she thinks I need to move up the ranks and become an administrator. I have no desire to do so, but it's all about status with her. Because she is always pushing me to do more and more, I never feel that I'm enough. This has caused me great heartache."

Performancism in Relationships

"Projects take priority over people; people are expected to wait."

"Relationships wilt from lack of care."

"Relationships aren't something you can check off your list and call 'done.' They take time. They're messy and unpredictable. People often just need you to be there for them, which feels like a waste of time for someone focused on performance."

Performancism at Home

"I'm at the stage where my kids need me so much, I can end up very dissatisfied with everything I didn't get done at the end of the day. I have to consciously remind myself of everything I did accomplish and let the rest go."

"I don't want my family to remember me as a stressed-out, crazy, rushing mamma and wife. I want them to remember us spending time together."

"Because of Facebook and Pinterest, I constantly compare myself to other women. Everyone else seems to be decorating their homes with artistically repurposed trash and cooking balanced meals with organic vegetables grown in their garden. I feel like I'm so far behind, I'll never catch up."

social media

Performancism at Work

"I practically kill myself to make sure I am seen as successful. Criticism and judgment crush me and make me angry because they undermine my sense of needing to be perfect."

"I feel desperate to receive recognition, title, applause, approval."

Performancism with Self

"Have I kissed my children today? Check! Fed everyone? Check! Read my Bible this morning? Check! Huge vacuum for the emotional aspects of these actions if we are just accomplishing them for the list, and that can lead to an extremely empty soul very quickly."

"I rarely allow myself time to rest or relax because there is always something I could be working on. It's almost as if I'm not super busy, then I'm not valuable."

"I expected all my achievements would protect me from pain. (They don't.)"

Performancism dangles satisfaction just out of our reach. "Do just one more thing..." he woos. But of course, when we finish that one thing, there's always "just one *more* thing." At the same time, Performancism brainwashes us to view relationships as time-wasters. According to him, it's only things we can check off our to-do lists that actually count in life. When we get tired and try to cut back, he tells us to quit slacking and do our part.

Are you as tired of this bully's carrot-and-stick routine as we are? If so, we're here to help you ditch your "human doing" status and reclaim your "human being" birthright.

CHAPTER 4

Procrastination

"I know I'm not enough, so why try?"

❋

Procrastination is a master of misdirection. If you start to wonder, *Am I so worried about the end product that I'm neglecting the process?* then Procrastination will quickly refocus you on the end product. He'll use a magnifying mirror that causes the end product to loom so impossibly large that you can think of nothing else.

Procrastination Defined

Procrastination is not the same as reflective thinking. Many of us need time to ponder important issues and choices.

Procrastination is not ignorance. When we don't know what we don't know, we can't even ask a question that would get us unstuck. This can look and feel like procrastination because we're not making progress, but it's not.

Procrastination is the practice of doing tasks that are less urgent but more fun before doing things that are more urgent but less fun.

Procrastination is sly. He never says, "I'm not going to let you do this." No, he takes a much more subtle approach. "Oh, you most certainly are going to do this. I know you will. You know you will. But now is not the right time. You certainly can't do it right now!"

Blogger Leo Babauta puts it this way: "We think it's OK to procrastinate, because we're going to do it later, for sure. Our future self will be incredibly productive and focused! Except, our future self is also lazy, and doesn't do it either. Eating chocolate cake is tastier, right now, than eating veggies."[12]

Procrastination comes up with urgent tasks that absolutely must be done before anything else. It reasons, "You certainly can't ____ when _____!" As in, "You certainly can't sit down and write when there are dishes in the sink!"

Of course, every important project has a critical moment, affectionately known as "the last minute." This is when we can probably pull off a good enough end product to prevent disaster: flunking the test, late filing penalties, getting fired.

"The last minute" is characterized by intense activity motivated entirely by fear. Once the cause for fear is gone—the consequence we're trying desperately to avoid—the motivation disappears and activity ceases. In this way, we allow Procrastination to systematically condition us to believe that the only time we get things done is when we're full of fear.

Over time, we buy what Procrastination is selling: the belief that we can be truly motivated *only* by fear.

Procrastination in Action

Every year, I (Cheri) assign several speeches to my students. And every year, many of them resist my instructions to brainstorm, write a first draft, practice with peers, revise, and practice some more.

"I'm just going to wing it," they tell me. "I do better off the cuff."

From two decades of teaching, and years of studying great presenters and stand-up comics, I've learned that anyone who looks like he's winging it has invested hours of effort into making his presentation or routine *seem* off the cuff. So in my classroom, nobody gets up front until he's gone through the full process.

When my students practice together, they make all sorts of startling discoveries. The opening story they thought would take thirty seconds drags on for five minutes. They haven't a clue what their main point is. They have no ending (other than "yeah," which doesn't count).

Procrastination removes the possibility of making these valuable discoveries. You have one shot, and whether it goes well or poorly, at least it's over. If it went well, you have evidence that winging it is, indeed, your thing. A poor performance becomes proof that you're no good at whatever it was.

The classes I've been taking in solo performing have given me an entirely new perspective on feedback and, thus, procrastination. I've written each of my monologues while participating in an eight-week workshop with seven other performers. During the first few weeks, we shared our ideas and asked for specific input from our peers. Initially, I was hurt to the point of tears when my peers and instructors didn't understand an idea I was trying to communicate. But as I kept wrestling with my ideas and revising my words, I discovered better ways to communicate. I felt exhilarated when one week they'd be shaking their heads in confusion at me and then nodding "I get it!" the next.

I've come to recognize that receiving feedback from people who care about me and are invested in my success is one of the greatest gifts I can receive. When my classmates said, "I don't understand," they weren't rejecting me, as I'd initially feared. They were really saying, "I care about you enough to be honest with you now so you'll be more effective on stage later."

After a performance, I'm always told, "I can't believe how far your piece has come!" My former, fear-based self would have heard this as condemnation: "You were so pathetic, anything would have been better than where you started." But my new, feedback-loving perspective allows me to hear pride and joy. My classmates and I thrive on giving and receiving honest input.

Procrastination short-circuits such a learning process. When we procrastinate, we tend to do what we've always done and get the same results we've always gotten. This means we're not growing.

Yes, procrastination lets us avoid the short-term pain of making that first attempt and facing the fact that it's mediocre, even lousy. It keeps us from experiencing the struggle to improve over time.

But in doing so, procrastination shields us from hope, as hope comes from struggle. Instead of feeling hopeful that we can improve, we resign ourselves to a lifetime of mediocrity, telling ourselves that extra effort is an exercise in futility.

The long-term effect of Procrastination that worries me the most is this: the belief that achievement really shouldn't take much time or effort. If speeches should be wing-able, then parenting should come naturally and marriage should be easy.

Expecting great results despite minimal effort is entitlement, pure and simple. And entitlement is an enemy of personal maturity.

How Others Perceive Procrastination

Of the three hundred women who responded to our "Women Trying to Measure Up" survey, two hundred considered themselves procrastinators. They felt that Procrastination shows up after Perfectionism, People-Pleasing, and Performancism have already ganged up on them.

When does Procrastination show up for you?

Procrastination in Marriage

"My ex-husband was a procrastinator but blamed it on 'waiting in faith' for things to happen. This was one of the factors that caused him to lose his family."

"Both my husband and I are procrastinators. We once ended up *spending twice the money* on plane tickets because we waited so long to buy them."

Procrastination in Parenting

"When my son procrastinates, it puts all of us on edge, and the result is normally lots of tears."

"As a mom, my kids' procrastination has caused me *many sleepless nights* staying up to help them type reports, gluing projects together, running to Walmart in the middle of the night for supplies."

"Both of my children are procrastinators and love putting off assignments until the last minute. This year it cost my daughter a scholarship because she waited until the last minute and didn't put her best effort into completing the application."

Procrastination in Relationships

"To me, it looks like the procrastinator doesn't care about me or what others need, just themselves and what they want."

"Procrastination makes you look irresponsible, untrustworthy, and unorganized."

"Procrastination causes a lot of tension and conflict in relationships."

Procrastination at Home

"Procrastination has made my house a disaster and led to self-loathing. I think, *How can I be so lazy and let this happen?*"

"Credit card and mortgage companies love procrastinators like me, because they get to collect late fees, fines, penalties, and interest."

"My sister struggles with procrastination that leaves her paralyzed in caring for her home. Sadly, I see this struggle being passed down to her children. They fear doing the wrong thing or being inadequate, so they fail to act at all. The consequence is *lack of growth*, resulting in *discouragement* and *defeat*."

"I put off housework and then get *embarrassed* when company drops in."

Procrastination at Work

"People's failure to meet deadlines means more work for me to do in less time under an extreme amount of pressure. IT IS NOT FAIR."

"Just today, my deadline for a project for church came due. I had two weeks to finish this project, and it would have taken me all of an hour if I'd done it right away. Instead, I put it off until last night...at bedtime. I didn't have everything I needed and ended up having to finish this morning. I was late to the meeting to deliver the finished product. Totally ridiculous!"

Procrastination and Self

"I end up exhausted and drained because I took a simple task and made it so much harder on myself than necessary."

"I find myself procrastinating when I have overcommitted myself. Then I become overwhelmed and can't focus on any one thing long enough to follow through and complete it."

"I used to procrastinate when I was afraid of something or afraid of failing. I would put it off until I seriously couldn't go through a single moment without it eating away at me and being in my every thought. I hated that feeling so much, I vowed not to live that way anymore!"

Procrastination is the most socially accepted of the bullies. Stories of pulling things off just in the nick of time make hilarious dinner party entertainment. But under Procrastination's good-natured smile is this sinister truth: he's just as deadly as his brothers. Steven Pressfield says, "The most pernicious aspect of procrastination is that it can become a habit. We don't just put off our lives today; we put them off till our deathbed."[13]

We don't want Procrastination convincing you to give up without a fight. We want you to discover, as we have, that "the process is the point."

Find the Joy

PART 2

How to Trade Try-Harder Living for Braver Living

※

Did one or more of the bullies seem frighteningly familiar to you? If so, you're not alone. When we speak about the four bullies of Try-Harder Living, women make a beeline to tell us, "Me too!"

We've talked with

- Stressed-out, overwhelmed women who are trying too hard to do too much.

- Discouraged, guilt-ridden women who feel like failures because nothing they do is good enough.

- Self-defeated, embarrassed women who over-promise but under-deliver.

- Resentful, isolated women who try to keep the peace and make everyone happy while their own needs go unmet.

- Dedicated women who sense a barrier between what they're doing and what God wants from and for them.

- Family and friends of women being beat up by the bullies of Perfectionism, People-Pleasing, Performancism, and Procrastination.

- New Christian women, taking their first steps on the path of spiritual maturity, who are anxious to do it all right.

- Spiritually mature women who publicly wear the "perfect Christian" persona while enduring the private torment of shame over secret struggles.

- Pastors' wives and female pastors who live under the microscope of the entire congregation, with every choice subject to criticism.

- Women in leadership roles that demand more and more, subtly eroding boundaries and balance in the name of doing the Lord's work.

- Women in ministry whose motto is "just try harder" as they try to camouflage the ineffectiveness caused by trying to be all things to all people.

- Stay-at-home moms who are urged by society (and even family members) to prove their worth by doing more than "just" raising the children and keeping house.

- Working mothers who feel guilty for leaving their children and try to make up for it when they're at home.

- Women in transition—due to a sudden life change (injury, illness, loss) or entry into a new season of life—who are wrestling with altered external and internal standards for measuring up.

- Women who serve as role models to youth and want to break free from the bullies instead of unconsciously teaching their beliefs to yet another generation of girls.

- Women who are (or have spouses who are) in the military, law enforcement, firefighting, EMT, and other fields that require perfection and performance to such a high level on the job that these demands spill over into personal and family life.

Do any of these women sound at all like you? How about some of your friends?

These women helped us realize that we have to rebel, because Try-Harder Living is killing us. We can't go on pretending it's not.

As you've seen in the previous chapters, Perfectionism, People-Pleasing, Performancism, and Procrastination aren't just harmless, lovable quirks. They're bullies with a death wish for each one of us.

But take heart. Their MO is predictable and obvious. And your weapon against them is the most powerful in all creation. You don't merely have a chance at beating them. Victory is guaranteed.

In Part 2, you'll discover why.

CHAPTER 5

Fear
The Main Force of Try-Harder Living

✳

I used to blame my calendar. It had such big empty squares. And I (Cheri) hated to see perfectly good space go to waste. Filling those squares gave me such a sense of satisfaction. Of course, I had to write in my tiniest print (and for the last few years, use reading glasses). But my plans sure looked good—on paper.

Then came the reality of living them.

The day I once considered my most stunning success as a multitasking human doing looked like this:

5:00 a.m.	Get up, dress, shower, do hair and makeup.
5:30 a.m.	Drive two hours to dog show.
8:00 a.m.	Ring time. She takes first place.
8:30 a.m.	Ring time. She takes reserve winners.
9:00 a.m.	Load up and head home.
11:30 a.m.	Arrive home where family and friends are preparing the house for daughter's fifth birthday party.
12:00 p.m.	Welcome guests to daughter's fifth birthday party.
3:00 p.m.	Leave house to buy supplies for evening sewing class.
4:00 p.m.	Arrive at class location. Set up sewing machines and cutting tables.
5:00 p.m.	Sewing class with eight participants who have never sewed before. Hustle to instruct, demonstrate, correct, fix, redo, rescue, and make sure each student heads home with a finished pair of shorts.
8:30 p.m.	Clean up and tear down.
9:30 p.m.	Arrive home, psyched that I pulled it off.

Now, there's a danger to sharing this: we overachievers are such a competitive bunch. You may be just itching to write me an email all about *your* best day. If so, you're reading me all wrong. I'm not sharing my crammed-to-the-gills day to impress you. Or make you think, "Wow, I need to step it up a notch!" I'm sharing this to show how the four bullies of Try-Harder Living can be calling all the shots while making us believe that we're still in complete control.

On the outside, I looked like I was waltzing through life with confidence, conviction, goals, and gusto. But what no one realized was that my every move was motivated by a nagging fear.

I was afraid of not being enough. I couldn't figure out how to *be* more. But I could *do* more. And I could *get* more.

At school, I ordered dozens of professional development books each year, expecting each one to transform me into "that" kind of teacher. With my own money, I purchased a SMART Board and iClicker system; surely they would do the trick!

I should have bought stock in Staples, I invested so much in office supplies. As if notecards, folders, binders, binder holders, colored tabs, electric staplers, and a heavy-duty three-hole punch would finally make me a good enough teacher.

At home, it was kitchen gadgets (to transform me into a mother who actually enjoyed cooking for her children), scrapbooking supplies (to force me to document memories), card-making kits (to make me into a thank-you-note-writing woman), shelves of books on spiritual disciplines (to turn me into a spiritual and disciplined person), and a full set of *Dance Dance Revolution* pads and DVDs (to help me get fit while having fun).

But no matter how much money I spent, I never bought enough to make me feel like I was enough. Instead, my ever-growing collections silently mocked me, highlighting my failures to become good enough as a wife, mother, and woman.

And the sad irony? If you'd asked me back then what I valued most, I would have been ready with the right answer: spending time with my family, creating a peaceful home, having financial security, and following God's call on my heart.

I had two mutually exclusive identities: the ideal one in my head and the real one I was living day to day. I didn't see how different they were. Nor did I recognize the damage my fear-driven choices were causing.

Reflecting on Values

My husband recently gave his high school seniors an ethics paper assignment. He asked them to outline their values and give specific examples. One girl came to him in consternation the next day. "Pastor G, I claim to value certain things, but the way I live is different from what I say I believe," she said. "Which should I write about—what I *say* I value or how I actually *live*?"

Do you find yourself in the same quandary: Knowing that in your heart you embrace one set of values, but finding that in your day-to-day life you're often living by other, perhaps more expedient values? Just for now? Until this crisis is over? Assuring yourself that when everything gets back to normal, you'll return to your core values again?

As you read through the following values list, circle *W* for anything you say with your words that you value and *L* for anything that your life consistently demonstrates that you value. In some instances, you will likely circle both:

1. W L   Using my abilities
2. W L   Taking risks
3. W L   Being a lifelong learner
4. W L   Treating people with respect and kindness
5. W L   Having fun
6. W L   Participating in hobbies and recreation
7. W L   Staying healthy
8. W L   Acting with personal integrity
9. W L   Living in the present
10. W L   Making a difference
11. W L   Reaching goals
12. W L   Experiencing career satisfaction
13. W L   Being a good steward of what God has given me
14. W L   Caring for the environment

15. W   L   Establishing financial security
16. W   L   Living a balanced life
17. W   L   Spending time with family
18. W   L   Enjoying intimacy with my spouse
19. W   L   Building a strong marriage
20. W   L   Loving God
21. W   L   Being a volunteer/participating in community service
22. W   L   Nesting and creating a home
23. W   L   Attending church
24. W   L   Reading God's Word
25. W   L   Being a good friend and having close friends

In the areas for which you circled both *W* and *L*, your stated values match your lived-out actions. You have integrity in these areas.

But what about those areas where you circled only one or the other? These are likely to be areas of conflict, stress, and anxiety. When you say that you value something but don't back up that belief with action, or you claim not to value something but participate in it, you live in hypocrisy.

Yes, we know: that's not a pretty term. It sounds awfully judgmental. But hang in here with us. We know that if we're pointing at you, three fingers are pointing back at us!

Did you know that the original meaning of *hypocrite* is "actor"? Someone who plays a part that isn't really her. That's what we feel like when we claim one set of values but live by another. Inauthentic. Phony. Fake. If you sometimes feel like you're living someone else's life, maybe it's because you are. Hypocrisy causes us to negate who we truly are— who God made us to be.

The Try-Harder Living bullies demand that we live according to priorities that we don't really believe in, and they cause us to violate the values we do. When we let them be our guides, they lead us off course, straight into deep, destructive behavioral ruts. Once in, we don't realize that we should get out.

How do they wield this kind of power over our lives?

They use fear.

The Bullies' Number One Weapon

Fear is at the heart of Try-Harder Living. As little girls, we each had our personal fear collections. Mine included snakes, spiders, strange noises at night, getting lost, scary men, and being laughed at.

But what are we afraid of now? Surely, as grown women, we've left far behind us childish fears about things that go bump in the dark, right? Yes and no.

I no longer scream when a student tries to startle me with a snake he's caught; instead, I say, "How beautiful!" and ask to hold it. I'm in charge of ridding our house of all insects and rodents. And I wear earplugs so nighttime noises don't bother me.

But I still hate being left behind. Daniel has learned the hard way not to wander away from me at Home Depot. I panic to the point of frantic searching and angry tears when I feel lost.

And don't get me started on scary men: those who yell, threaten, refuse to listen, dismiss my feelings, or treat me with contempt. When I feel a man is unsafe, my knee-jerk reaction is to run, run, run—the farther and faster the better.

I love to evoke laughter when speaking or performing. But if I feel like someone is mocking me, I stiffen into a statue as my stomach tightens, my ears buzz, and my temples throb.

Universal Fears

We all experience these fight, flight, or freeze instincts. And while your individual set of panic-button pushers is unique, we are all susceptible to four universal fears.

1. Fear of Pain. Pain includes physical and emotional, actual and anticipated, my own and others'. A friend's unexpected criticism hurts my feelings. My back tenses up as I think about the cramps that will hit in a few hours. I feel my child's disappointment over not making the team as if it were happening to me.

2. Fear of Loss. The threat of loss permeates our lives. Most obvious is death: losing my own life or losing someone I love. Loss of a dream can feel like a small death. I know what it's like to lose my health; to feel perfectly fine one minute and be ushered into a year of agonizing pain the next. I've lost more relationships than I care to count—many due to moves, some to irreconcilable differences, and a couple when BFFs suddenly decided they hated me.

3. _Fear of Blame_. "It's all your fault!" is the clarion call of blame. When hit with blame, I juggle and pass it on as fast as I can. I fear being blindsided by the fallout from accidental mistakes; I fear discovery when I've knowingly done something wrong. Guilt and shame typically come along with blame.

4. _Fear of Shame_. Shame is the sense that I am not worthy of love and belonging. Shame tells me that not only am I alone in this world; I deserve to be left alone. I am simultaneously "too much" and "not enough"; I am defective. I haven't just made a mistake; I _am_ a mistake.

One Rebel's Story

My friend and fellow rebel Adelle Gabrielson shares how fear held her hostage when she was a new mom:

> When my first child was about two years old, there was another mom new to the area with a son the same age who tried incredibly hard to be friendly with me. She suggested play dates—I snubbed her. I avoided her if I saw her coming at church. She was trying to be nice. But I was so miserable and pathetic and full of working-mother shame that I was convinced we could never be friends.
>
> Would you like to know why?
>
> She was pretty. And skinny. And well-dressed. _And_ she was a stay-at-home mom. Maybe I could have been friends with a plain stay-at-home mom, but one that looked just like Cinderella? Nope.
>
> To avoid the potential pain of rejection or being disliked, I would pigeonhole people from the get-go, deciding first if they would like me or not, without ever giving the friendship a chance. _How could someone like her possibly enjoy the company of someone like me?_
>
> How many friendships have I missed because of this paralyzing fear of not being enough? Perhaps this other mom needed my friendship desperately, but I was too blind to see beyond my own irrational fear.

Fear paralyzed Adelle, causing her to miss out on much-needed friendship.

Fear persuaded me to cram my calendar squares and clutter my closet shelves.

Fear enslaves us to the bullies, compelling us to behave according to their beliefs instead of our stated values.

CHAPTER 6

Love
The Core Choice of Braver Living

✳

Love is at the heart of Braver Living.

The last line of this familiar Bible verse about love used to terrify me (Cheri): "There is no fear in love. But perfect love drives out fear, because fear has to do with punishment. The one who fears is not made perfect in love" (1 John 4:18).

The harder the THL bullies pushed me to make myself perfect, the more fear-filled I became. So I heard the phrase "the one who fears is not made perfect" as condemnation, straight from the Word of God, that I was beyond all hope. I was so encompassed in fear that this verse, intended to help me overcome fear, actually had the opposite effect.

The truth is, God wants to unlock the chains of fear, freeing us from its power.

The New Living Translation offers a slightly different interpretation of 1 John 4:18, which I find compelling and comforting: "Such love has no fear, because perfect love expels all fear. If we are afraid, it is for fear of punishment, and this shows that we have not fully experienced his perfect love."

So fear isn't proof that I'm hopeless for not making myself perfect. Fear is simply a warning sign that indicates I've not fully experienced God's perfect love.

What a difference!

If the core issue were our failure to become perfect, then the solution would be to keep trying harder. Exactly what the Try-Harder Living bullies want us to believe. But since the real problem is our failure to fully experience God's love, the solution has nothing to do with trying harder. And everything to do with fully experiencing God's love.

Experiencing and Responding to God's Love

While there are myriad ways to experience God's love, we're not going to take a bag of tricks approach. We're going to stay focused on the core choice *we* make when living braver: love.

The word *braver* means "possessing or exhibiting more courage." *Courage* comes from an old Latin word meaning "heart." So Braver Living is all about heart: fully experiencing God's heart of love for you and responding by loving God with all your heart:

> "The most important [commandment]," answered Jesus, "is this: 'Hear, O Israel: The Lord our God, the Lord is one. Love the Lord your God with all your heart and with all your soul and with all your mind and with all your strength.' The second is this: 'Love your neighbor as yourself.' There is no commandment greater than these" (Mark 12:29-31).

The more we love God, ourselves, and others, the more fully we experience God's love.

Love God

We love God by actively *believing* Him and actively *obeying* Him. How? Jesus spells it out clearly for us in John 13:34-35: "A new command I give you: Love one another. As I have loved you, so you must love one another. By this everyone will know that you are my disciples, if you love one another."

How do we actively love God? "If you love me, keep my commands" (John 14:15).

When we obey God, what do we demonstrate? "Whoever has my commands and keeps them is the one who loves me" (John 14:21).

If we love God, what will we do? "Anyone who loves me will obey my teaching" (John 14:23).

How will we fully experience God's love? "If you keep my commands, you will remain in my love" (John 15:10).

What command are we to obey? "This is my command: Love each other" (John 15:17).

Love Myself

Loving myself isn't about developing super-sized egos or becoming puffed up with pride. God's command to love ourselves recognizes that the degree to which we love (or don't love) ourselves profoundly influences our ability to love others. We can't give away what we don't have. If we're full of self-hatred, we can't give love. If we're full of fear, we can't give respect. We can give only what we have.

"Oh," you might say, "I'm just harder on myself than anyone else."

This sounds great in theory. But when your child hears you muttering, "You are such an idiot!" when you've made a mistake, how safe is she going to feel coming to you when she's messed up? And when your spouse hears you chewing yourself out because "You did the same dumb thing again! Why don't you ever learn!" how likely is he to approach you to ask for forgiveness for the same old problem?

And when it comes down to it, who has to listen to your badmouthing self-talk the most? You do. As women, what we hear we take to heart. And "what you say flows from what is in your heart" (Luke 6:45 NLT). Which means that our self-slamming becomes a perpetual cycle of negativity: out our mouths, in our ears, into our hearts, and back out our mouths.

It's not okay to hate on ourselves. And telling ourselves that our self-abuse doesn't impact others does not mean it doesn't impact others. It does. If you don't believe us, ask someone who loves you how they feel when they hear you putting yourself down. Their answer may surprise you.

Loving myself means first *believing* God when he says that I am…

- right with God, pure, holy, redeemed (1 Corinthians 1:30)
- a new person with a new life (2 Corinthians 5:17)
- brought to fullness in Christ (Colossians 2:10)
- loved, chosen, holy, and blameless (Ephesians 1:4)
- freed and forgiven (Ephesians 1:7)

- God's handiwork (Ephesians 2:10)
- bold and confident (Ephesians 3:12)
- chosen and appointed (John 15:16)
- justified, free from the penalty of sin (Romans 3:24)
- not condemned, belong to him, freed from the law of sin and death (Romans 8:1-2)
- more than conquerors, loved (Romans 8:37)
- inseparable from the love of God (Romans 8:39)

Loving myself also means *obeying* God. Obedience starts with lots of listening. It's the only way we can tell the difference between God's voice and the voices of the Try-Harder Living bullies, not to mention our own internal chatter and all the other people clamoring for our attention.

The more we learn to hear God's voice and take him to heart, the better we will understand what he's leading us to do.

Love Others

The Try-Harder Living bullies con us into believing that love is a feeling that comes naturally, especially to women. We just can trust our instincts, run with our female intuition. We don't need to learn how to love others, and we certainly don't need practice. Love just happens; anything that involves work can't be love.

In fact, if we find ourselves struggling to love someone, the bullies let us completely off the hook. Some people, they assure us, are just impossible. We can't possibly be expected to love them.

God makes it clear, through his Word and his own deeds, that love is an act of the will. Regardless of how we feel, loving others means *believing* what God says about them. This is hard. It's much easier for us to believe what we're currently thinking about them:

- "She's so bossy."
- "He's so stubborn."
- "She's so frustrating."

Love is a conscious choice to remember that what God says about us, he says about others too:

- She is complete in Christ (Colossians 2:10).
- He is God's masterpiece (Ephesians 2:10).
- She is victorious and loved (Romans 8:37).

Loving others also means obeying what God asks us to do for them. This also takes effort, as we typically have our own ideas of what we should (or shouldn't) do.

Instead of spouting off, "I'm just going to give her a piece of my mind!" God asks us to give "a gentle answer" (Proverbs 15:1). Rather than deciding, "I refuse to deal with him," God asks us to "live in harmony with one another" (Romans 12:16).

Loving others means choosing to avoid the bullies' relationship advice and listen to God's guidance for Braver Living.

One Rebel's Story

Jesus promises that making the Braver Living choice to love will enable us to receive his gift of peace: "Peace I leave with you; my peace I give you. I do not give to you as the world gives. Do not let your hearts be troubled and do not be afraid" (John 14:27).

In this tale of two visits shared by fellow writer Shauna Letellier, notice which home involved troubled hearts and which was characterized by peace.

> I always thought it was respectful to have a perfectly clean house for guests. It was a badge of honor declaring me a "Perfect Hostess."
>
> I'd knock myself out to earn that before company came, and I always felt gratified when someone slapped that badge on my lapels with the words, "Wow! Your house is so clean!"
>
> Until I went to a girlfriend's house who practiced the same neurosis. Her house was spotless, and yet she couldn't stop apologizing for the places it wasn't. I was there for coffee and a play date, but I was terribly uncomfortable. I didn't

want my kids to leave fingerprints on countertops or foot-
prints in freshly vacuumed carpet.

When it was time to leave, I got all nerved up cleaning
up toys—literally sweating and annoyed that my toddlers
weren't joyfully helping out. I left in a sweating panic wondering if I had relaxed or not.

In contrast, I had coffee with another friend later that
year. There were piles of mail on her desk, a used mixer on
the counter, flour and measuring cups in the sink, and a
warm coffee cake on the table. She relaxed at the table and
enjoyed my company.

When it came time to leave, I went upstairs to organize
the horrifying mess. Toy bins tipped over, play food scattered from room to room. I almost started hyperventilating.

She followed me upstairs, laughed at the catastrophe,
and forbid me to pick up one toy. Then she helped me get
my kids' shoes and coats on. I left feeling relaxed and blessed
by a friend who knows how to host.

Since then, I have done less neurotic preparation and
sought to enjoy my company instead of my clean house.
And when I do, I apply a new badge of honor to my own
lapels: "Peaceful Hostess."

Peace is the litmus test, indicating whether our choices are driven by
fear or motivated by love.

CHAPTER 7

Take the First Brave Steps

✳

In this chapter, you're going to take two very brave steps: finding your stated values and facing your lived values. We encourage you to find a Bravery Buddy to do this with, someone who will support you, be honest with you, pray with you, and hand you chocolate at all the right moments. And you, of course, can do the same for her.

Got one? Great.

(Need one? Check out our Facebook page!)

Checking Reality

But first things first. In the spaces below, we urge you to make a list of

Five recent commitments you said yes to and why.

1. _____
2. _____
3. _____
4. _____
5. _____

Five recent projects you started or joined and why.

1. _____
2. _____
3. _____
4. _____
5. _____

Five detailed things you did.

1. _____
2. _____
3. _____
4. _____
5. _____

Five recent tasks you postponed.

1. _____
2. _____
3. _____
4. _____
5. _____

Finding Stated Values

Now, with these lists in mind, complete each of the following statements by checking all options that reflect your motivations.

I say yes because:

_____ I can't say no.

_____ I want to avoid conflict.

_____ I feel guilty if I say no.

_____ I generally find a way to get out of it later.

_____ I'm afraid someone will ask me why if I say no.

_____ they need someone.

I focus on details because:

_____ there's no such thing as an insignificant detail.

_____ nobody else seems to care about them.

_____ I hate looking incompetent.

_____ I'm terrified of making mistakes or failing.

_____ they distract me from dealing with the big-picture issues in my life.

_____ I *have* to. I can't not.

I get involved in new projects because:

    ____ it makes me feel good to join or start something new.

    ____ I love the sense of momentum.

    ____ I like to bury myself in busyness.

    ____ I'm a get-it-done kinda gal.

    ____ I hate doing nothing.

    ____ I'm more comfortable as a "human doing" than a "human being."

I put things off until later because:

    ____ I prefer immediate gratification, something that will give me a quick reward now.

    ____ I get caught up in the paralysis of analysis.

    ____ sometimes I really don't care if they get done or not.

    ____ the task seems so huge that I have no clue how to approach it.

    ____ I'm not the kind of person who asks for help. Ever.

    ____ I get stalled out partway through a project and can't get going again.

I take on new commitments before:

    ____ praying for guidance.

    ____ seeking input from the stakeholders in my life.

    ____ evaluating my time and energy available prior to, during, and after the commitment.

    ____ asking questions to make sure I understand what I'm agreeing to.

    ____ discussing contingencies for changes in the project or my life.

    ____ defining boundaries for what I will and will not do (i.e., saying yes to whatever they imagine I've said yes to).

Now go back through and write an *F* beside each checked option that represents a choice you make out of fear rather than love.

Facing Lived Values

So, the bad news first. The more motivations you marked as fear-driven, the more you've bought into the values of the Try-Harder Living bullies: creation and maintenance of an image.

But don't despair; you're not alone. We know what it's like to make check after check on these lists wondering, *How on earth did I get here? When did I pick up all these habits? How do they happen without me even realizing it?*

And if you're feeling miffed, maybe even a bit angry, as if you've been duped and are just now finding out? You're in good company, girlfriend.

We get it. We know what it's like to try hard to be good, to do our best, to put others first, to glorify God only to discover that we've been doing a lot of the right things for all the wrong reasons, and even in a lot of wrong ways.

So here's something you need to know right now: *It's not your fault.*

You didn't ask to get beat up by the Try-Harder Living bullies. You didn't know you'd been conned into accepting their beliefs. It's easy to feel betrayed, as if you don't know which way is up or down any more. Or who you can trust.

We get that too.

And if you start to panic that now you'll have to unlearn dozens of bully beliefs that have taken you a lifetime to get straight so that you can start learning all the new beliefs instead…

Take a deep breath. We've also gone through this. Multiple times, in fact.

Here's something else you need to know: *Your life is about to get a lot simpler.* We aren't saying easier. We can't say easier, because the journeys we're sharing with you have required some of the hardest work we've ever done. But we promise this: as you say farewell to Try-Harder Living and welcome Braver Living, everything really will get simpler.

You'll stop feeling like a marionette with dozens of strings jerking you every which way at once. In fact, as you embrace Braver Living, those strings will break one-by-one as you walk free of the bullies.

Until everything—every choice, every decision, every option, every commitment, every action, every word—comes down to simply you and Jesus.

You and Jesus.

A New Vision

Would you like a glimpse of what your life will look and feel like as you stop trying harder and start living braver? Go through these statements, circling *D* for those you already do and *W* for those you want to do.

I say yes when:

D W   I sense God calling me.

D W   I can do so honestly.

D W   I really want to be a part of it.

D W   I'm ready to commit all the way to the entire process.

D W   I have thought through the reasons why I can and will.

D W   I recognize that I am needed.

I focus on details when:

D W   they'll make an important difference.

D W   God will be glorified.

D W   quality will benefit everyone.

D W   they'll help me learn and grow.

D W   I'm being honest about dealing with big-picture issues.

D W   I choose to.

I get involved in a new project when:

D W   I've finished my previous projects.

D W   I've had enough rest since finishing my last one.

D W   I'm sure I'm not using it as an escape from my problems.

D W   I'm clear that it's worth doing.

D W   It's a choice, not a compulsion.

D W   my unique contribution will make a difference.

I postpone taking action when:

D W   I sense a check in my spirit.

D W   I realize that I might be disguising meddling as helping.

D W   I need time to reflect before reacting or responding.

D W   other steps need to come first, such as prayer, discernment, planning.

D W   I need to seek counsel or ask for help.

D W   I need more information to make a wise choice.

I take on a new commitment *only after*:

D   W   praying for guidance and receiving clear direction.

D   W   seeking input from the stakeholders in my life and having them all on board.

D   W   determining that I have enough time and energy prior to, during, and after this commitment to devote to it and everything else I'm already committed to.

D   W   asking enough questions to be certain that I fully understand what I'm agreeing to.

D   W   including contingencies so that if there are changes to the project or in my life, my agreement may change as well.

D   W   setting clear boundaries regarding what I am and am not committing to in time, energy, finances, and other resources.

These are just some of the choices that characterize Braver Living. So celebrate your *D*s and get ready to make progress on those *W*s!

Braver Living in Action

Let's close this chapter with a couple of concrete examples of how my life changed as I (Cheri) started Living Braver.

In late 2013, I filled out the application, wrote a check, and addressed the envelope for a series of five weekend retreats I've been wanting to attend for several years. As I'd penciled the dates on my master calendar, I'd noticed that at least two of the dates conflicted with prior commitments. But I wanted to attend the retreats so badly that I did what I've always done: I told myself, *You'll find a way to make it work.*

But before mailing the envelope, I felt convicted that I was once again buying into the bad beliefs of the Try-Harder Living bullies rather than making a careful, prayerful choice consistent with my stated values. Later that day, after tearing up the envelope, I posted this to my Facebook status:

> Cheri Gregory is erasing several penciled "I'd love to do this" events from my early 2014 calendar and throwing away the brochures/sign-up forms. Slowly learning that wanting to DO everything can be a form of greed that's every bit as insidious as wanting to HAVE everything.

The immediate responses were both telling and validating:

- "Amen!"
- "That is a stellar observation."
- "Ohhh…good insight! Thanks for sharing, feeling an aha moment!"
- "I can understand this perfectly…I actually collect experiences."
- "Super awareness! Thanks for sharing, as it totally helps me to see the same in my life!"

I didn't expect my one Braver Living choice to have such a ripple effect. But following through on my shaky resolve actually helped other people recognize that they were being driven by Try-Harder Living too. Five days later, I posted this:

> Loading up the Murano with yet another wave of decluttering giveaways, I hear a familiar condemning voice insinuate, *You should feel ashamed of yourself for wasting money on all this stuff in the first place.*
> For once, I know how to respond: *No. Shame is what got me into this mess in the first place. Grace is getting me out. I choose to feel grateful. And I'm finding what it's like to feel free.*

This time, I was struck by the transparency of the responses.

- "Amen! And bless you!"
- "How encouraging! Love that!"
- "You have that same voice in your head? Thanks for the encouragement."
- "Thank you for that—now I know the script."
- "Way to go, Girlfriend! Cleaning out some things, myself! Woo hoo!"
- "Yay, YOU! The Number One Reason I don't get rid of junk is the shame I feel over acquiring it and warehousing it in my home. That's no longer a good enough reason."

- "The lightness of heart when we let go is unbelievable, isn't it? There is so much freedom in letting go. You go, girl!"

- "I've had the same guilty voice…thank you for sharing a response!"

- "Interesting timing…so far, in the past three weeks, I have donated one full carload of stuff, taken out roughly forty bags of garbage, and have two carloads more ready to donate. I love how you said shame got you there and grace gets you out. I've been feeling sick to my stomach over how much we have that we don't care to keep. Talk about a lesson in needs vs. wants. I apparently had it all wrong. None of this stuff filled the void, healed the pain, or satisfied the craving."

In sharing my own rebellion against Try-Harder Living, not only did I encourage others to recognize the bullies beating them up, but I shared some tools to help them join the rebellion too.

Who would have thought that a girl who's believed the bullies most of her life would end up leading a band of rebels?

CHAPTER 8

What Type of Rebel Are You?

✳

In any battle, we want to know as much as possible about the enemy forces. That's why we spent time learning how to identify the four Try-Harder Living bullies and recognize their signature strategies.

Before charging into battle with your flag held high, you ought to know as much as possible about yourself too. What assets and liabilities do you bring to the rebellion? What natural talents do you have and what training will you need? What danger zones should you be aware of? What can we count on you to always do—and never, ever do?

Most importantly, knowing your rebel personality helps you strategize toward victory over the Try-Harder Living bullies.

Discovering Your Rebel Type

For each scenario, circle the one response that is most true for you. If two are equally true, circle them both. (You can also take this assessment online at www.TheCureForThePerfectLife.com.)

1. In childhood photos, I
   - E) am always smiling and posing.
   - AN) am sitting up straight with a serious look on my face.
   - D) have an "Are we done yet?" look that conveys what an interruption the photo shoot was to my plans.
   - AM) slouched, leaned, laid all the way down, or hidden behind someone or something.

2. When board games come out at a party, I
   - E) want to play and be part of the group.
   - AN) know, follow, and enforce the rules.

D)   play to win.

AM)   enjoy watching others play.

3. When it comes to a dreaded project or chore, I

E)   try to turn it into a game.

AN)   like figuring out exactly what needs to be done and doing it all correctly.

D)   get a thrill from checking it off as yet another item done on my to-do list.

AM)   often dink around until it's too late or someone else has already done it.

4. When there's a sudden change of plans, I

E)   may be devastated (if the change makes me feel disappointed) or elated (if the change makes me feel anticipation).

AN)   will be distressed because what I'd counted on happening is not happening and I may attempt to reverse the change and make the original plan happen after all.

D)   react in frustration, even anger, to the loss of control.

AM)   patiently roll with it—"It is what it is."

5. If I had a day of free time, I would love to

E)   get together with friends and family for a spontaneous party.

AN)   reorganize a closet, a room, the garage, or the entire house.

D)   start or finish a new project.

AM)   "chillax."

6. When developing a relationship with a new boss (or other authority figure), I

E)   try to get to know him and make him laugh.

AN)   analyze his expectations and strive to meet them.

D)   challenge him, testing his right to be in charge.

AM)   try not to attract any attention for the wrong reason.

7. When it comes to my clothing choices, I am drawn to

E)   eye-catching colors and prints.

AN)   coordinated outfits in subdued hues.

    D)   functionality.

AM)   comfort.

8. If my flight were to be delayed by five hours, I would want to

    E)   talk to all the interesting people hanging out in the airport with me.

AN)   catch up on my reading.

    D)   make progress on a project via my laptop and cell phone.

AM)   find a quiet place to catch a nap.

9. If a stranger were to watch me for a week, she would conclude that I highly value

    E)   playing.

AN)   organizing.

    D)   doing.

AM)   resting.

10. I learn best by

    E)   talking, active discussion, debate.

AN)   seeing, visualization, diagrams.

    D)   listening, repeating aloud, hearing audiobooks/videos/podcasts.

AM)   getting hands-on, making a model, demonstrating a process.

11. If I were to enter a competition and do poorly, the worst part of the entire experience for me would be

    E)   disappointing others; not giving them something to cheer about.

AN)   making mistakes; trying to figure out what I'd done wrong.

    D)   not being number one.

AM)   all the stress of the entire experience.

12. When learning a new skill, the thing that upsets me the most is

    E)   corrections.

AN)   illogical instructions.

    D)   failure to progress rapidly.

AM)   complexity.

13. The worst part for me about being sick is
    E)   being isolated from people.
    AN)   the germs, messes, and medications.
    D)   the to-do list that's not getting done.
    AM)   not feeling well enough to actually enjoy the R & R.

14. Behind my back, I'm pretty sure people say that I'm too
    E)   talkative.
    AN)   obsessive-compulsive.
    D)   bossy.
    AM)   lazy.

15. In school, my response to a group assignment was typically
    E)   euphoria that I could receive class credit for socializing.
    AN)   resignation that I would be the one to make sure the finished product was good enough to turn in.
    D)   determination to make sure everyone did their part rather than just getting a free ride on my efforts.
    AM)   satisfaction that there were plenty of other people in the group to make sure it got done (and usually at least one of them was far more invested than I was).

16. I consider someone a bad driver if he
    E)   honks at me or makes a rude gesture.
    AN)   doesn't follow the rules of the road, thus endangering the safety of others.
    D)   drives slowly in front of me rather than pulling over to let me pass.
    AM)   causes an accident.

17. I am likely to find it difficult to respect an authority figure who is
    E)   critical.
    AN)   late.
    D)   incompetent.
    AM)   insensitive.

18. My biggest time management issue is

    E)   optimism: I act as if everything will magically work out (and, if not, who cares if I'm a little late?).

    AN)   deciding a project is "done enough": I get so caught up in little details that projects often remain unfinished.

    D)   energy management: I start too many projects and try to do them all simultaneously.

    AM)   breaking a large project into smaller steps: I focus on the expected end result and get so intimidated that I put it off, often until it's far too late to actually do it at all, let alone well.

19. An important contribution I make to my friendships and to my family is demonstrating how to

    E)   really enjoy life.

    AN)   care about quality.

    D)   get things done.

    AM)   live at peace.

20. If our family were to plan a trip together, they would rely on me for _____ (but then _____)

    E)   spontaneous enthusiasm and tons of excitement (but then I might forget to pack half the necessaries).

    AN)   alphabetized checklists for packing (but then I might become stressed from double-checking all the pre-travel details).

    D)   leadership in setting concrete goals for the trip: where to go, what to see, how long to stay (but then I might tire every one else out with a demanding daily agenda).

    AM)   a calm and easygoing presence, with a bit of dry humor that breaks any tension (but then I might dig in my heels right at the worst possible moment).

21. Others would describe my walk as

    E)   strutting.

    AN)   pacing.

    D)   striding.

    AM)   sauntering.

22. When checking in to a hotel, I
    E)   tell the person behind the counter all about why I've come to town and ask for restaurant recommendations.
    AN)   ask for a room that's away from traffic and noise.
    D)   pray for no line and quick service.
    AM)   hope the bed is comfortable.

23. Of the following, the one I find most distressing is
    E)   rejection.
    AN)   chaos.
    D)   powerlessness.
    AM)   disharmony.

24. If I were asked to help plan a friend's birthday party, I'd want to
    E)   welcome guests as they arrive and get them involved in mixer games.
    AN)   make sure the invitations are accurate and include a map.
    D)   order the food and decorations.
    AM)   show up and help however.

25. When my plans don't turn out the way I'd expected, I'm likely to respond
    E)   with disappointment shortly followed by a better new plan.
    AN)   with days of letdown and wondering why this always happens to me.
    D)   by blaming whoever messed up my plan.
    AM)   by making fewer plans.

Now, add up your totals:
    (E)   Expressive = _____
    (AN)   Analytical = _____
    (D)   Driving = _____
    (AM)   Amiable = _____

Your highest score correlates with your dominant personality type, and your next highest score indicates your secondary type.

If you're learning about your personality type for the first time, we're delighted to be introducing you to these ideas. This information has given us many lightbulb moments about ourselves and our relationships.[1] Now let's take a look at what type(s) of rebel you are.

The Expressive Rebel

The Expressive Rebel's Idea of Victory: when she's enjoying relationships with others

The Expressive Rebel's Top Emotional Needs:

attention

affection

approval

The Expressive Rebel's God-Given Assets:

talkative, storyteller	cheerful and bubbly
life of the party	curious
good sense of humor	good on stage
memory for color	wide-eyed and innocent
emotional and demonstrative	sincere heart
enthusiastic and expressive	always a child

The Expressive Rebel's Potential Liabilities:

compulsive talker	blusters and complains
exaggerates and elaborates	naïve and gullible
dwells on trivia	loud voice and laugh
cannot remember names	controlled by circumstances
scares people off	seems phony to some people
too happy for some people	never grows up
egotistical	

The Expressive Rebel's Danger Zone: When an Expressive is overstressed, she naturally slides toward People-Pleasing.

Not all Expressives Fall Victim to People-Pleasing

Since victory for an Expressive is when she's enjoying relationships with others, it's easy to assume that all Expressives are people-pleasers. After all, to enjoy relationships, you not only need people, but you need people who are pleased to be with you. It's a guaranteed setup for People-Pleasing, right?

Not necessarily.

When an Expressive lives a Spirit-led life, she functions primarily out of her assets, sharing her natural gifts. Her core identity does *not* include the unending neediness, unrealistic expectations, resentment, bitterness, or martyrdom of the People-Pleaser.

When an Expressive dominates a conversation, telling all about herself and her life, it's easy to assume that she's doing nothing more than getting her attention fix.

But Expressives can teach us a vital life skill: *vulnerability*. Expressives long to connect with others, to know and be known. What can seem like too much information (TMI) to non-Expressives is often their way of initiating a deeper relationship. The stories they tell often have the deeper message, "I've shown you some of my dirty laundry...will you risk showing me some of yours?"

Whenever my mother and I (Cheri) heard a speaker share the messy parts of her life story, my mother's reaction was always, "How can she say *such things* in public?" She believed that skeletons belonged in closets.

But I have always been drawn to such speakers. When I was a teenager, they were my lifelines. The fact that they shared the hard, hurting parts of their lives gave me hope for the pain I was experiencing. They gave me hope that I would not have to keep silent about my secrets forever.

I'm not saying that every word spoken by Expressives is a rare gem; they can spout plenty of fluff. But they also model admirable qualities of openness and trust.

The Analytic Rebel

The Analytic Rebel's Idea of Victory: when she's achieved and maintained excellence

The Analytic Rebel's Top Emotional Needs:
sensitivity
support
space

The Analytic Rebel's God-Given Assets:

deep and thoughtful	appreciative of beauty
serious and purposeful	sensitive to other people
genius-prone	self-sacrificing
talented and creative	conscientious
artistic or musical	idealistic
philosophical and poetic	

The Analytic Rebel's Potential Liabilities:

remembers the negative	selective hearing
moody and down	self-centered
enjoys being hurt	too introspective
false humility	guilt feelings
off in another world	persecution complex
low self-image	tends to hypochondria

The Analytic Rebel's Danger Zone: When an Analytical is stressed, she most naturally slides toward Perfectionism.

Not All Analytics Are Driven by Perfectionism

Since the life goal of the Analytic is to achieve *and* maintain excellence, it's easy to assume that all Analytics are perfectionists.

Not so. When an Analytic lives a Spirit-led life, she functions primarily out of her assets, sharing her natural gifts. Her core identity does *not* include the anxious, frustrated, relentlessly critical, dissatisfied spirit of the perfectionist.

This isn't to say that your Analytic sister won't sigh when she finds a dirty dish in the sink or arrange your spices in alphabetical order the moment you turn your back. But her motivation may not be at all what you think.

Non-Analytics (especially those of us who are especially sensitive to criticism) can pass harsh judgments on their behaviors. And we are often wrong.

I (Cheri) learned this the hard way with my mother. For decades, I took every tsk-tsk she uttered under her breath as a stab in my heart, proof that she did not love and accept me for who I am. I now understand that my mother's drive for excellence sprang from her idealism. Because she loved me so much, she wanted to provide the absolute best for me. When she couldn't, it pained her.

Her sighs and tsk-tsks were not aimed at me; they were aimed at a world that never matched her ideals. Her perpetual disappointment expressed her longing for heaven, where she knew everything would *finally* be just right for the daughter she loved.

The Driving Rebel

The Driving Rebel's Idea of Victory: when she is initiating change

The Driving Rebel's Top Emotional Needs:
   achievement
   appreciation
   loyalty

The Driving Rebel's God-Given Assets:

born leader	not easily discouraged
dynamic and active	unemotional
compulsive need for change	exudes confidence
must correct wrongs	can run anything
strong-willed and decisive	independent and self-sufficient

The Driving Rebel's Potential Liabilities:

bossy	will not give up when losing
impatient	comes on too strong

quick-tempered	inflexible
cannot relax	not complimentary
too impetuous	dislikes tears and emotions
enjoys controversy and arguments	is unsympathetic

The Driving Rebel's Danger Zone: When a Driver is stressed, she naturally slides toward Performancism.

Not All Drivers Are Controlled by Performancism

Since the life goal of the Driver is to initiate change, it's easy to assume that all Drivers are performancists—that they're robotic "human doings" rather than "human beings."

Not so fast. When a Driver lives a Spirit-led life, she functions primarily out of her assets, sharing her natural gifts. Her core identity does *not* reflect the driven, domineering, desperate crazy-busyness of performancism.

Non-Drivers often find the fast pace and high productivity of Drivers intimidating. They assume that Drivers

- know that others find them intimidating

- intimidate others intentionally

Both assumptions are often wrong.

A Driver working in her strengths sees the big picture and strives to make a difference. She notices a problem and seeks to solve it. Immediately. She sees something not working and fixes it. Stat. She realizes that "the way we've always done it" is no longer relevant and lobbies for change. Pronto.

Prolonged analysis and contemplation in committees drives a Driver crazy because she wants to do something now. Not in ten years or ten months. Drivers are optimists who see new visions for how things could be and take the shortest routes there.

The Driving Rebel has a kingdom vision in her heart as she charges forward. She initiates change so that

- pain will be relieved.
- suffering will end.
- hunger will be satisfied.
- thirst will be quenched.
- children will be protected.
- women will be safe.
- prisoners will have hope.
- the marginalized will have advocates.
- the silenced will have voices.

The Amiable Rebel

The Amiable Rebel's Idea of Victory: when she's in a place of peace

The Amiable Rebel's Top Emotional Needs:
respect
self-worth
harmony

The Amiable Rebel's God-Given Assets:

low-key personality	quiet but witty
easygoing and relaxed	sympathetic and kind
calm, cool, and collected	keeps emotions hidden
patient and well-balanced	happily reconciled to life
consistent life	all-purpose person

The Amiable Rebel's Potential Liabilities:

unenthusiastic	selfish
fearful and worried	too shy and reticent
indecisive	too compromising
avoids responsibility	self-righteous
quiet will of iron	

The Amiable Rebel's Danger Zone: When an Amiable is stressed, she naturally slides toward Procrastination.

Not All Amiables Are Held Hostage by Procrastination

Since the life goal of the Amiable is to be in a place of peace, it's easy to assume that all Amiables are procrastinators. Unmotivated. Lazy. Enough with the labels.

When an Amiable lives a Spirit-led life, she functions primarily out of her assets, sharing her natural gifts. Her core identity does *not* reflect the undisciplined, self-indulgent, escapist spirit of Procrastination.

You may find yourself wanting to light a fire under the Amiables in your life. You may feel convinced that their inaction is nothing more than a passive-aggressive control tactic. But we can learn the value of slowing down, and even pushing pause, from the Amiable Rebel.

Amiables teach us how to be present. Not regretting the past, not reaching for the future, but living in the now. They teach us to notice the people around us and treat everyone with respect and dignity, regardless of who they are. Amiables teach us how to stop for a spell. To "be still" so that we can know he is God (and we aren't). They teach us that taking refuge is a prerequisite to seeking strength.

Amiables teach us to take time away before going back into the fray.

A Rebel Must Wear Her Own Glasses

Think of each personality's natural way of seeing the world as her own pair of monochromatic sunglasses. She doesn't see all colors, just a particular spectrum incredibly well.

Personality "masking" occurs in childhood when we are forced to put on another personality's glasses for self-protection. We feel that we must perform key behaviors of the masked personality to keep an authority figure happy. For example,

- an Expressive wearing her Analytic mother's glasses, stressing herself to the point of an eating disorder to get straight *A*s.
- an Analytic wearing her Expressive father's glasses, dragging herself to parties and telling pre-practiced stories to

make everyone laugh, only to return home exhausted and miserable every time.

- a Driver wearing her Amiable mother's glasses, denying her gifts of influence by turning down invitations to lead and staying safely behind the scenes wondering why she feels so lethargic.

- an Amiable wearing her father's Driver glasses, overcommitting and underdelivering, letting everyone down, ultimately feeling like a pathetic disappointment.

<u>Wearing glasses that aren't our own distorts our vision</u>. Without our specific monochromatic lenses, we lose sight of our own victory goals and personal assets. And because the borrowed glasses are a different color, we can barely see well enough to perform a few key tasks of our borrowed personality.

Worse yet, along with the borrowed glasses come all of the liabilities of the personality they actually belong to. We start expressing a host of weaknesses that aren't even ours.

For example, since I (Cheri) wore my mother's Analytic glasses as a child and teen, I am very skilled at buying colored hanging file folders, matching plastic tabs, blank inserts, and setting up perfectly organized filing systems. How do I know such behavior is evidence of my Analytic mask rather than my true personality?

- First, I loathe the process. Unlike an Analytic, who feels a sense of satisfaction while organizing, I feel completely persecuted.

- Second, once I set up such a filing system, it's of no use to me. I can't find anything ever again. Once I put a sheet of paper in a file folder, it's lost and gone forever!

- Third, I start setting up filing systems as a stall tactic, not as a useful part of a healthy organizational process. I pour time and money into setting up beautiful folders, which typically do nothing but gather dust.

The longer I wore my mother's Analytic glasses, the more my Expressive assets were replaced by Analytic liabilities. My humor was replaced by self-deprecation, enthusiasm by skepticism, friendliness by self-centeredness, creativity by overplanning, spontaneity by hesitancy, and forgiveness by grudge holding.

I wasn't *really* an Analytic; I was just masking. But the longer I wore Analytic glasses, the more blind I became to my true Expressive self. In fact, when I was admitted to the eating disorder unit of a neuropsychiatric hospital at age seventeen, I was diagnosed with "a profound lack of a sense of self."

The Try-Harder Living bullies are behind this whole "wear the wrong glasses" scheme. Nothing makes them happier than a woman who has no idea who she is. That means that they get to help her discover herself by—you guessed it—creating and maintaining an image. First they blind us and then convince us that we see better than anyone else. It's diabolical.

Forcing the perspective of one personality on another is one of the surest ways to invite the bullies into both lives. One of our strongest defenses against the bullies is keeping our glasses on and allowing others to wear their own too.

When we respect each other's perspectives and work together, we become a formidable rebel force.

PART 3

12 Cures for the "Perfect" Life

※

It's time to get messy and see what all of this looks like in everyday real life.

Speaking of messy, while writing this book, we invited some of our friends to contribute stories. One especially apt story arrived with the following apologetic email:

> It's 11:30 at night. I'm tired, I'm struggling, and everything I type sounds awful when I read it back. Having said all of that, here's my submission.
>
> I don't know if it's good. In fact, I'm thinking it might be pretty random, but I'm trusting that your awesomeness will take whatever I've attempted to write and make it into something brilliant.
>
> If you end up not wanting to use it, I totally understand. If it's not what you were looking for, just dump it in that digital garbage can.

We were thrilled with the story and immediately wrote, "We love it!" back to the contributor. As we did so, we realized that many of the contributions came with similarly self-deprecating, unsure disclaimers, such as:

- "If you can't use it, I totally understand!"
- "I'd like to revise this if you decide to use it."
- "I can go back to the drawing board if this isn't what you need."

While we appreciate the humility and teachable spirit displayed by each contributor, we also recognize two other powerful forces at work here.

First, the bullies clearly had a heyday, both with the women who contributed and those who thought about contributing but didn't.

Second, the women who contributed made choices of incredible bravery. In spite of the fears aroused by Perfectionism, People-Pleasing, Performancism, and Procrastination, they chose to write. They chose to hit "send."

Each woman who hit "send" made the risky choice to give us a glimpse into her heart, without knowing how she and her story would be received.

And here's the irony: for all the concerns these women felt about their writing, we didn't need perfect writing. Writing is fixable; that's what revision and editing are for. All we needed from each woman was authenticity.

Authenticity is what it takes to battle the bullies.

Simple? Yes.

Easy? Not so much.

12 Bully Beliefs We've Bought Into

Perfectionism, People-Pleasing, Performancism, and Procrastination bully us into buying many beliefs that keep them thriving at our expense. Together, we're going to explore and refute these twelve bully beliefs:

1. If I want something done right, I'm gonna have to do it myself.

2. If I can't do it right, I won't do it at all.

3. I don't do angry.

4. Everything I feel is valid and must be valued.

5. No fun until my work is done.

6. I'll rest when I'm dead.

7. I'm responsible for everyone else's happiness.

8. I am what I do.

9. I can't throw it away; I might need it someday.

10. I work better under pressure.

11. I got myself into this mess, so I have to get myself out.

12. *No* is a dirty word.

Some chapters will hit home with you more than others. For the ones that don't really feel like they apply to you, here's a suggestion: try reading them to better understand someone in your life who does struggle with that particular bully belief.

So, are you ready to do battle with the Try-Harder Living bullies in the everyday ordinaries of your life?

Forth into the fray!

CHAPTER 9

Redefining "Right"

There's more than one right way to do things right.

✳

Before you wonder, "Am I doing things right?"
ask, "Am I doing the right things?"

ANONYMOUS

Bully belief 1: "If I want something done right, I'm gonna have to do it myself."

"What's that?" I (Cheri) asked Daniel, ransacking each grocery bag for what I clearly wrote on the grocery list: garlic.

"It's elephant garlic. I thought it looked interesting, and we could try something new!" he said, holding out an obscenely large, grey lump.

We are not trying something new in my vegetable soup. I'm making it for a potluck, so it needs to taste exactly the way it's supposed to. I heaved an intentionally audible sigh and continued my inner monologue. *Why did I say yes when he offered to help? If only I'd gone to the store during my lunch break. Not only do I have to act grateful for elephant garlic, but I also have to figure out how to get my hands on nice, normal garlic.*

As always, *the only way to get anything done right around here is to* do it myself!

Reflecting on Your "Rights"

Now perhaps you're thinking, "I would never get bent out of shape over something as silly as elephant garlic. In fact, if someone did the grocery shopping for me, I'd sing the Hallelujah Chorus."

Okay, so maybe elephant garlic isn't your challenge. But take a moment and check off any of these scenarios that hit closer to home:

1. ____ When I'm visiting someone else's home, I often straighten pictures on the walls when nobody's looking.

2. ____ I avoid criticism by going above and beyond.

3. ____ I compliment others only when they've done something deserving of praise.

4. ____ When I make a mistake, I say (or think), "What is wrong with you?...How could you be so stupid?...Can't you just get it right?"

5. ____ If I had a child who brought home a report card with all *As* and one *F*, I would focus on an immediate plan to solve the *F*.

6. ____ I feel compelled to correct people in conversation (pronunciation, grammar, accuracy of facts).

7. ____ When visitors come to my home when it's not been properly cleaned, I can hardly think about the people, I'm so fixated on the dirt.

8. ____ I feel physically ill when plans turn out wrong or my house gets messy.

9. ____ People regularly disappoint me and let me down.

10. ____ I can't sit and relax when I know there are urgent matters to do or fix.

11. ____ I tend to check and recheck details for complete accuracy.

12. ____ I do my best to make sure failure is never my fault.

13. ____ When people say I'm being defensive, they should just let me explain so everything would make sense.

14. ____ I resent people who gush, "You're so good at everything!" to my face but label me "anal-retentive" behind my back.

15. ____ I can't help it that I am better at some things than most people.

16. ____ I love my lists; I hate being "listless"!

Now go back through the list and erase any checked scenarios that you know, in your heart of hearts, are motivated by love and result in peace for you and others in your life. Keep any scenario checked if it describes an action or reaction that springs from fear. How many still have checkmarks?

Perhaps you would never get all bent out of shape over something as silly as elephant garlic. But when it comes to the scenarios you've left checked, here's the truth, girlfriend: *It's all elephant garlic.*

One Rebel's Story

My hysterical friend Jenny Sulpizio, author of *Confessions of a Wonder Woman Wannabe,* shares her experience with this first bully belief that "if I want something done right, I'm gonna have to do it myself":

> I'm supposed to be in recovery—notice I said *supposed* to be. However, every now and then (and despite all of my good intentions), I lose my willpower, fall off the wagon, and succumb to my perfectionist ways of old.
>
> The thing is, as a recovering perfectionist, I know the triggers—whether it's something I see on Pinterest, Houzz, or in a magazine while I'm waiting in line to get my oil changed—my tendencies for all things perfect like to rear their ugly head. Often. Especially around Christmas.
>
> And this year was no exception.
>
> After deciding on the color scheme for our Christmas decor, I couldn't wait to get to trimming my tree and decking my halls. The burlap ribbon, the rustic ornaments, and the cute adornments I had just purchased were sure to make this year's celebration the best ever. My goal? To replicate those perfectly dressed trees I'd seen beautifully displayed at the various department stores. The problem? My kids asked to help.
>
> Now, I can't believe I'm going to admit this to you, but I actually took issue when it came to displaying my kids' ornaments on our tree this year. Ugh. Indeed, my desire for all things perfect had gone a little too far, as my judgment grew cloudy and my reality had been tampered with. Instead of embracing the ornaments my children had lovingly made throughout their years in school, I mistakenly saw them as a nuisance—because they didn't fit into the design I had envisioned for my tree.
>
> Seriously? Who does that?

Me. I do that.

And I'm going to venture to guess that I'm not alone. Well, at least I hope I'm not.

Because no matter how hard some of us try, we still fall prey to our tendencies—to our perfectionist ways. We get caught up in our visions, and our ideas of what holidays, birthdays, and every other day should look like. We compare. We yearn. And then we turn into some sort of evil creature when we don't get our way—when something messes with our ideas and our propensities towards all things perfect.

And let me tell you—it ain't pretty. At all.

Bully belief 1 lures us into believing we are right. *Only* we are right. *Always* right. It makes it hard to consider that we might be "Wr...Wr... Not exactly right."[1]

Or, at least, that others might be right too.

Surprise! There's More Than One Right Way

When I (Cheri) was fourteen, I volunteered as a Big Buddy for five-year-old Suzie, a cancer patient at the local hospital. One day, Suzie declared, "I'm going to draw a tree!" and grabbed a purple crayon.

Purple? I have no artistic talent whatsoever, but I know that drawing a tree requires two colors, and neither one is purple. Purple. Who ever heard of a purple tree? True to my Driver personality, I reached over, yanked the purple crayon out of her hand, found the brown crayon, and thrust it at her.

Suddenly, I saw my supervisor beckoning to me. She invited me to join her on the far side of the room, where she spoke in a conspiratorial whisper. "What if we...let her draw a purple tree?"

I stared back at her. *Let her draw a purple tree? Of all the audacious, impudent, bold ideas. We could let her draw a purple tree. Yes! Yes, as a matter of fact, we could.*

I marched back across the room, snatched the brown crayon out of Suzie's hand, and quickly replaced it with the original purple crayon, announcing victoriously, "You can draw a purple tree!"

For the first time in my life, it occurred to me that my way might not be the only way.

God Offers a Different Right Way

God beckons us, inviting, "What if *we*…"

> Even so the body is not made up of one part but of many… in fact God has placed the parts in the body, every one of them, just as he wanted them to be. If they were all one part, where would the body be? As it is, there are many parts, but one body. The eye cannot say to the hand, "I don't need you!" And the head cannot say to the feet, "I don't need you!" (1 Corinthians 12:14,18-21).

I've wasted decades and damaged many relationships living as if I, on my own, am the body. My attitudes and behaviors have said far more clearly than words, "I don't need you!" to my husband, my children, my friends, and my students.

God wants us to expand our tunnel vision. To become open to others' points of view. To recognize the value of their ideas, thoughts, and preferences. To actively seek their input rather than relying solely on our own perspectives.

God is clear: we do need each other.

How to Right Wrong Priorities

When I read on Patty Newbold's blog, *Assume Love*, that expecting others to meet my standards of right is nothing short of "premeditated resentment," my first response was, *Ouch! I resemble that statement.*

"I don't mean to tell you what to do, but…" rolls so effortlessly off my tongue. The bumper stickers on my life proclaim, "If it's worth doing, it's worth doing right," and "My way or the highway." Learning to stop fixating on how I think things should be done and start opening up to other options has been a slow process.

If you're struggling with the same tendencies, here are two simple (but not necessarily easy) steps that can help develop greater openness:

1. Seek Confirmation that You're Doing the Right Things

When you're hyper-focusing on what you feel you must do, it's easy to get trapped believing,

- "I have to do this."
- "This must get done now!"
- "Nobody else understands how important this is."

You can question such rigid beliefs by asking,

- "Why do I feel that I have to do this?"
- "Could this get done another time just as well? (Or possibly not at all?)"
- "Why is this *so* important to me?"

When you can't come up with good reasons for what you're doing, it's a red flag that you're being driven by fear. And if you're at all like me, you throw your relationships under the bus when fear is at the wheel.

When I got upset with Daniel for buying elephant garlic, he assured me that my potluck soup would taste just fine with elephant garlic or no garlic. That made me even more upset with him for not understanding my needs. But when I paused to question my reaction, the best I could come up with was, "I have to do this because I have to do this."

At that point, I faced a choice between two rights: following a recipe right or treating my husband right.

The one key choice of Braver Living reminds us that love wins over fear any day.

2. Expand My Definition of Doing Things Right

When you're feeling hyper-vigilant about the right way to do things, you may be unintentionally sending messages like these:

- "Your ideas aren't as good as mine."
- "I don't care about your feelings, just mine."
- "Deal with your own needs."

You can develop greater openness by actively practicing curiosity:

- "Who might be able to suggest new ideas?"
- "I wonder how she feels about this?"

- "Which of his needs are going unmet in this situation?"

Yes, you might need to grab a paper bag to hyperventilate into as you ask these questions. I'll be glad to loan you one of mine. Letting go of control is hard. But according to the key choice of Braver Living, it's right.

As you recognize that your thoughts and actions are being governed by Bully Belief 1, practice openness with this new mind-set: "I'd rather be happy with others than 'right' alone."

Choose Happiness over Being Right

What might this new mind-set look like in action during everyday life situations? (By which I mean nonemergency, nonabusive circumstances involving personal preferences and opinions.) Here's one example of a time I chose to hold my tongue, pray for guidance, and make a choice out of love rather than cave in to my craving for self-rightness.

Daniel told me he needed printer ink. When I asked him to give me an empty cartridge, he gave me the item number, saying he'd looked it up online.

Oh, how I wanted to buy the right ink. And I wanted to get it right the first time. I wanted to tell him, in no uncertain terms, to march to his printer, pull out an empty cartridge, and hand that puppy over.

But for too much of our marriage, I'd fought for my rights at every turn. My criticizing and cajoling had gotten me whatever I'd wanted in the moment, while destroying what I most desired: a close, loving relationship with my husband.

So with ink-cartridge number in hand, I prayerfully weighed my choices: Do things right or do the right things? Insist on being the entire body or do my part?

Convicted that in this situation the right thing for me to do was to simply buy the ink, I purchased all four cartridges. (Although I was sorely tempted to get only one, just to be sure.)

Days later, when Daniel opened the box, he spluttered in frustration. "Would you believe this isn't even the right ink? I looked it up...the computer said it's supposed to be..."

Oh, how appealing doing things right the first time still felt. And oh, how tempted I was to say, "If you'd given me an empty ink cartridge like I'd asked you to, not only would you have the right ink, but I wouldn't be listening to your bellyaching right now."

But I remembered: I'd rather be happy with others than right alone. Giving voice to self-righteous thoughts wasn't going to make either of us happy or bring us closer together. So I said nothing.

Daniel, on the other hand, stayed upset with himself. In fact, he was ultimately harder on himself than I would have been.

Several days later, as we drove home from Staples with the right ink, I shared my whole inner struggle with Daniel. He agreed that he'd put me in a no-win position. More significantly, he thanked me for making the choice to respect him and let him learn his lesson the hard way rather than insist on my way.

That day, God led me to stop sacrificing my relationships on the altar of my rightness.

Since then, I've been convicted to make a variety of choices in similar circumstances with various people. Sometimes, I've said, "If that's how you'd like it done, go ahead and do it" in a nondefensive voice. Sometimes I've said, "You know what? I'm going to double-check" with a wink and a smile. And sometimes I've kept quiet. Each time, making the key choice of love kept relationships a priority over my own sense of rightness.

When faced with a conflict between being right and demonstrating respect in a relationship, seek guidance by praying, *Am I focused on doing things right or doing the right things?* and *Am I insisting on being the entire body or am I doing my part?* Then be open to the Holy Spirit's conviction and leading.

Choose Learning over Being Right

I grew up believing a dangerous corollary to bully belief 1: Being wrong is the worst thing in the world.

In my childhood home, all struggles were kept secret. This produced the paradoxical expectation that I would avoid taking risks while still producing the right results every time. I grew up expecting the impossible: that I'd learn without failure, achieve mastery without mistakes, grow without struggle.

I was Exhibit A of what happens when being wrong feels like the worst thing in the world: "The child may come to believe failure is something so terrible, the family can't acknowledge its existence. A child deprived of the opportunity to discuss mistakes can't learn from them."[2]

I didn't just have to be right, I was driven to be right—or at least look right—all the time. Since it's not possible to be right all the time, I resorted to a lot of blaming and hiding. I missed out on a lot of valuable learning.

According to Daniel Coyle, author of *The Talent Code*,

> Much of the research about learning and the brain could be distilled into a few simple words:
> Mistakes are good. Struggle makes you smarter.
> When it comes to applying this lesson to our lives, the problem is not with the science, but rather with our powerful natural aversion to mistakes and struggle.
> Try as we might to convince ourselves otherwise, mistakes feel crummy; struggle feels like a verdict. Also, mistakes often carry a social price. They can cost us our job, our money, our pride. So we instinctively hide them.[3]

I tried band for a week but quit because I was no good (translation: I couldn't get every note right on the first try). I was too self-conscious to try out for choir. I spent twelve years taking piano lessons, but my terror of making public mistakes doomed me to disaster at every recital.

But I had one friend whose life contradicted both Bully Belief 1 and its corollary. The way Carlyn took risks, you'd think she'd never even heard of always being right and never being wrong.

"I'm going to teach you to water ski," she declared early in our friendship. I told her that she could try all she wanted, but I wouldn't be able to learn. She laughed at my nonsense.

"You're doing great!" she insisted weeks later as I swam toward the boat, mortified from a dozen falls in my first half hour of trying. After two more hours of trying and falling, I finally popped up on a single ski. As I glided across the water, my victory grin mirrored Carlyn's.

Carlyn taught me that being wrong isn't the worst thing in the world; it's a normal part of the learning process. She showed me that partnership and collaboration are worth far more than being right and alone.

Carlyn was my first Bravery Buddy. She knew how to make learning safe. Without pressure to be always right and never wrong, I was free to struggle and grow.

If you wish you had a Bravery Buddy right about now, start by being your own. Remind yourself that "Right" is often the enemy of "Done." That your way is one of many right ways. That being wrong isn't the worst thing in the world, but failure to learn and grow just might be.

As you stop trying harder to be right and start living braver, you'll make learning safe for yourself. You'll become a safe person for others to learn with. And one day, you'll look around and see that in becoming a Bravery Buddy, you're surrounding yourself with other Bravery Buddies.

You'll realize that as good as it feels to be right, brave relationships feel even better.

Tiny Acts of Rebellion

1. I will thank someone for doing something I don't want to do, so I'll get in the habit of noticing and appreciating others' gifts.

2. I'll find a class on something I've always wanted to learn but have been too afraid to try.

3. I'll create a sign that says, "Mistakes are good; struggle makes you smarter," and put it somewhere I'll see it often.

4. I'll start following a blogger who writes about grace, such as Ann Voskamp or Emily Freeman.

5. The next time I'm faced with a choice, I'll try to imagine how each of the four personality types would approach it. This will help me remember that my perspective isn't the only one around.

Tips for Each Rebel Type

Expressive

You have an optimistic view of yourself and love to dive into new projects with enthusiasm. Even though you're not naturally detail-oriented, you are sure that with the right equipment and a little help from Pinterest, you'll figure it out in no time. Your inborn social nature means that you're more likely than some to collaborate, but you tend to shy away from including Analytics because you perceive their observations as critical.

Analytic

Bully belief 1 feels like truth for you. Since being right and doing things the right way are such automatic priorities for you, it's easy to assume that you're always right and that if others would just listen to you, they could be too. It's hard for you to avoid saying, "I told you so" when others do their own thing and later wish they'd listened to you. Keep in mind that "we do our worst sinning when we're right" if we allow rightness to take priority over treating people with love.[4]

Driver

You like to do things your way; nobody needs to agree with you that it's the one right way, but they'd better not tell you it's the wrong way! You dislike delegating because of all the messes you've had to mop up after people who proved less competent or motivated. Although it takes a lot longer to teach others than to simply do a task yourself, equipping others pays off in the long run. One of the greatest roles you can assume as a leader is that of mentor; your efforts and reach will be multiplied.

Amiable

You feel that doing things right is a rather arbitrary, even overwhelming expectation. If you could just concentrate on one task at a time, perhaps. But since life seems so full of so many things vying for your attention, and multitasking is not your strong suit, striving to do them all right is not likely to be a goal on your radar. Just keeping your head above water seems like a laudable goal for now.

CHAPTER 10

Perfect Is for Pinterest

How to stop striving for perfection and actually get things done.

✳

"Fail quickly and get it over with."
KEN DAVIS

Bully belief 2: "If I can't do it right, I won't do it at all."

I (Kathi) am sure the phrase, "If you can't do something right, it's not worth doing at all," was first said by a picky mom to a child who responded, "Okay, then, fine—I won't do it at all."

The intention behind the saying was certainly honorable: Don't do a sloppy job. Do the best you can to your ability.

But some of us didn't hear the intention behind those well-meaning words. Some of us heard: "If you know you can't do it perfectly, don't even try." And it has screwed us up ever since.

While Cheri tends toward the "I'll work till I'm dead to make this project the best that it can be" side of this rule, my mind goes to "It's probably not going to be good enough, so why even bother trying in the first place."

Here's how my brain works:

If I can't clean the whole kitchen, why get started at all?

I only have fifteen minutes to work on cleaning out my email, and that will barely scratch the surface. I'll just wait until I have more time.

I won't work out this week because I'll be gone for a couple of days. I'll wait until next week when my schedule calms down.

So instead of making slow progress on things, I tend to wait until company is coming over and mad-dash-clean, answer my email when people start to wonder if I've been involved in a serious car accident and have lost all use of my hands, or spend extra time at the gym before my weigh-in at Weight Watchers.

I have Perfectionistic Paralysis: I would rather do nothing than do something to less than the best of my ability.

How We Pre-disqualify Ourselves

Are you paralyzed by Perfectionism? Circle *T* for those statements that are true about you or *F* if they are false, and then total up your number of true responses.

1. T   F   When a friend tells me my bra strap has been showing for hours, I am appalled at her for not telling me sooner and at myself for letting it happen.

2. T   F   Affirming someone for doing their best is silly; results are what count.

3. T   F   I've been told that I tend to be an all-or-nothing thinker.

4. T   F   I don't like learning a new skill where others can see me try and fail.

5. T   F   I have creative abilities (painting, singing, writing, etc.) that I've not shared with anyone because I'm sure people would just tell me I'm wasting my time.

6. T   F   I'd rather get an *F* for not trying than invest my best efforts and still fail.

7. T   F   Criticism crushes me. I'll do anything to avoid it.

8. T   F   If God wants me to do something or become something, it will just happen.

9. T   F   I agree with the wisdom of Yoda: "Do, or do not; there is no *try*."

10. T   F   I dread letting down the people I care about.

11. T   F   "If at first you don't succeed, try, try again" doesn't work for me; I need to succeed the first time, every time.

12. T   F   Being talented or gifted means being good at something naturally, without having to work at it.

13. T   F   I know that God has called me to do specific things for him, but I'm so afraid of letting him down that I haven't even tried.

14.　T　　F　　If I won't win, I won't play.
15.　T　　F　　I make long to-do lists and then freeze because I don't
　　　　　　　know where to start.

An ideal score here is 0 true, 15 false. The more of these statements that are true for you, the more likely it is that you, too, get frozen by Perfectionistic Paralysis.

I was reading the memoir/manifesto of Facebook COO Sheryl Sandberg, *Lean In: Women, Work and the Will to Lead*. In one of the chapters about why women try less often than their male counterparts for management jobs, she revealed this fascinating statistic about the company my husband works for: "Internal research by Hewlett-Packard found that women only apply for jobs for which they feel they are a 100 percent match; men do so even when they meet no more than 60 percent of the requirements."[5] I couldn't believe it and shared that stat with Roger, adding, "Why would anyone apply for a job that they were only 60 percent qualified for?"

"Oh, I've done that," Roger said. "I'm guessing some of the jobs I've applied for I was probably only 40 percent qualified for."

My husband is one of the smartest, most capable men I know. So what was he doing applying for jobs he wasn't completely qualified for?

He continued. "Yeah, if it's something I'm interested in, I can figure it out as I go along. Where better to learn than on the job?"

And the crazy thing is, nine times out of ten, he's gotten the job. And he's done great work each and every time.

It got me to thinking. *How many times have I missed an opportunity because I felt that familiar feeling, "Why would they want me anyway? It's better not to waste my time trying than getting everything prepped and ready only to be disappointed in the end."*

This all-or-nothing thinking keeps us from the jobs we would love to try but feel unqualified for, the friendships we'd like to pursue, and the projects we want to tackle.

Perfectionistic Paralysis: The Flip Side of "Just Try Harder"

If the Try-Harder Living bullies can't sucker us into trying hard to do things perfectly, they are happy to switch from, "Just try harder" to "Don't even try."

Think of this silly scenario: You know you need to clean out your pantry—it's impossible to find anything in there, there's a bunch of expired food that you will never use, and the shelves could use a good wipe down. You could probably do the job in under a half hour, but instead, if you're a perfectionist like me, you figure you shouldn't do it until you really, *really* have time to do it right.

So you wait.

And every time you go to the grocery store, you shove a few more boxes on top of the old ones and figure you'll go through the old ones later.

Eventually that pile really does feel daunting, and a job that could've taken a half hour now takes hours. And leaves your entire kitchen a disaster. And leaves you feeling totally distraught.

Perfectionistic Paralysis strikes in two different ways.

1. Before You Start

THL says, "Avoid the Pain."

Recently, I had an email I needed to send. One that had been at the bottom of my email folder for two weeks. Not an expired Bath & Body Works coupon, this was a business email that needed a thoughtful response.

I'd had some not so pleasant back-and-forth with this person, and I just wanted to avoid the pain. The problem? The pain made its way to the surface of my life every time I opened my email program.

Finally, I had to realize that by not answering this email, I was causing myself more pain than whatever this woman could throw at me. Instead of avoiding pain, I was just drawing it out over a longer period of time.

Try-Harder Living tells you, "You're not ready to open that email—do it later. It will be easier later." But we all know that's a lie. As with any other decision or action, the longer we wait, the heavier it gets.

THL says, "You're going to fail anyway, so why even waste your time?"

If you postpone starting a project because you're thinking of all the ways it could go wrong, you may be suffering from a fear of failure. Fear of failure is motivated by how we look to other people. If you get the feeling, "I don't want to look stupid to other people," this is a fear of failure talking.

THL says, "This will just mean more work later on."

And then there's the other side of the fear coin. You may be paralyzed by the thought that if you do this task well, you are no longer under the radar and now others will have a higher expectation of you.

In my early twenties, I filled in for our church secretary for a week while she was on vacation. I could figure out most of the tasks that were assigned to me except one—the fax machine. I couldn't figure out how to replace the empty roll of fax paper. (Yep, this was an old-school fax machine.) The only other person working there at the time was the senior pastor, so I asked him how to change it.

"I don't know and I don't want to know," he said. "As soon as I learn how to replace the fax paper, I'll be the one responsible to do it every time."

So I ended up calling the regular secretary on her vacation and asked her how to do it. Turns out, it was easier than changing a roll of toilet paper.

This incident is an extreme example of someone not willing to learn something new so that nothing new would be expected of him.

Can I just say that is an awfully limiting way to live?

THL says, "This is too big!"

I spent a month having the same item on my to-do list—and it was only a fifteen minute project: "Write fifteen minutes on chapter four." Simple enough, right? So why did I spend weeks avoiding it?

Because it felt big. I knew I needed to go through some files to actually find chapter four, and when I finally found it, I didn't remember what was already written. Would I be pleasantly surprised on how much work I'd already accomplished? Probably not. My mind turned to fear and doom at the looming task.

What I had here was really two tasks: 1. Find and open the file. 2. Write for fifteen minutes. Once I realized it was two tasks, it felt doable—like I was getting a check mark for each of the things I was actually doing.

Try Harder Living

2. When You've Stalled Out

THL says, "Aren't we there yet?"

"If I were doing this project right, it would be done by now!" Or "Other people could have done this better than I have. I should just give up and let someone who would do it better take over." It's easy to believe our first impressions of a project—that everything will rise up to meet us. But just because it's hard and there are more obstacles than we first imagined, doesn't mean that we're wrong; it just means that it was harder than we thought.

THL says, "You don't have everything you need!"

It will probably take time and energy to find everything again, figure out the passwords, get the supplies together, whatever. Often we've put it away in such disorder that untangling the mess feels worse than starting over.

THL says, "You're stuck."

Sometimes, it's easy to get started. There is all the enthusiasm of getting things rolling and the dream of what the outcome is going to be.

When I start writing a new speech, I'm excited because I have a couple good ideas, and I am pumped to get started. But then I start looking for what I don't have—a great illustration or a great quote—and then I start to lose interest because it's not fun and easy anymore.

It happens on any kind of project: I get partway in and need something I either don't realize I need or can't get my hands on. Or it turns out that what I thought were going to be easy steps turn into difficult obstacles.

THL says, "You can stop feeling the pain—now!"

When we start a project, we have all the confidence in the world—there are only possibilities and victories ahead. But then we run into things we don't understand or people saying no. That's when doubt and uncertainty set in.

Your brain starts to protect you from pain. It tells you, "It's too big! Stop now!" If you just put it off, you can stop feeling pain. And we hate pain...and it's easy to forget all that confidence we had up front.

A Perfectionistic Paralysis Parable

Jesus told a parable about a businessman who gave money to three servants before leaving on a trip. To one, he gave five bags of gold; to another, two; to the last, one. The servants who had received five and two bags of gold invested and doubled their master's money. The servant who had been given one bag of gold just dug a hole and hid it.

When the businessman returned, the first two servants showed off their earnings and were rewarded with praise and privileges. But the last servant said,

> "'Master...I knew that you are a hard man, harvesting where you have not sown and gathering where you have not scattered seed. So I was afraid and went out and hid your gold in the ground. See, here is what belongs to you.'
>
> "His master replied, 'You wicked, lazy servant!...You should have put my money on deposit with the bankers, so that when I returned I would have received it back with interest.
>
> "'So take the bag of gold from him and give it to the one who has ten bags. For whoever has will be given more, and they will have an abundance. Whoever does not have, even what they have will be taken from them. And throw that worthless servant outside, into the darkness, where there will be weeping and gnashing of teeth'" (Matthew 25:24-30).

This is convicting. I've heard this parable so many times, but I never thought about it as an illustration of the fear of not being perfect keeping us from doing what God wants us to do.

Did the servant with the five bags take a risk? Yes. But that was the only way he reaped the reward.

I think a lot of people feel like they aren't burying talents when they are just putting them off, but the truth is that if you aren't using them now, you're not using them.

God is telling us not only to stop ignoring our talents, but to stop postponing our talents. Stop waiting until you're fearless—you never will be—but do as much as you can with what you have. That's brave living.

Getting Unstuck

Here are a few ways to avoid getting stuck when Perfectionistic Paralysis starts to set in.

Break the Task into Smaller Bites

So many times I feel like I need to sit in my chair and get everything done or I've failed. But we need to realize that sometimes the right way to do a task is not to finish but simply to start.

Email is one of the easiest things for me to procrastinate on. If you have too many emails sitting in your inbox, it's overwhelming. Here is my system for handling emails (no matter how many I have).

1. Figure out how many emails I have.

2. Set a target. When my email is out of control (Just returning from a vacation or poking my head up after the completion of a big project), I set a reasonable number to get done in a set amount of time. All of us need a target to aim for. Let's say my target is to deal with 25 emails this afternoon.

3. Break 'em down. Not all emails are created equal. I have three categories of email:

Easy. These are the emails that just need to be filed—in email folders or in the trash—and emails that just need a quick, one-sentence response. ("Sounds great! Thanks!" or "Let me send a quick note to Diane to check on that.") Most emails fall into this category.

Medium. These emails require a thoughtful response or need some research before I can respond, such as: "What is the name and address of the person hosting the party we're going to next week?" or "Can we set up a time to talk on Monday?" Those may seem like simple emails, but sometimes I avoid them because they can get me sidetracked.

Hard. This is any email that is going to take more than five minutes to answer. "Can you get me a report on that new medical plan?" or "Honey, can you follow up with the insurance company on our claim?" You know those emails. The tiny little ones that require a bunch of work. Those big hairy projects can be so overwhelming that I don't even want to get started because I know they're going to be a bear to complete.

So if I have 25 emails, I will break them down this way:

Easy: 20

Medium: 4

Hard: 1

That way, I can zip through the easy emails, spend a few minutes on each of the medium emails, and set aside some time for the one hard email. I give myself a checkmark in each category as I complete the email. In my mind, I'm giving myself some extra credit for getting those medium and hard emails done, instead of letting them languish at the bottom of my inbox.

How this helps: Instead of telling myself, *Kathi, stop being a baby. It's just email. Suck it up and do it* (which rarely works on me or other people), I'm acknowledging that it's going to take some time. Some of the tasks are going to require more than a passing glance, but I will have an emotional reward at the end: 25 emails. Gone.

This is a system for email, but it can be applied to almost any chore that feels overwhelming: cleaning the kitchen, pulling together a presentation, trying anything new. Break it down by difficulty or time segments.

Give Yourself Rewards

I am all about self-bribery.

Writing is very hard for me. (I know, I chose a great profession, right?) I love the feeling of having written something (notice the past tense there), but actually sitting down to a blank page? Totally overwhelming.

So I break it down as I mentioned above, but then I also set up rewards for myself: If I write a thousand words, I can spend twenty minutes on Facebook. Another thousand words? I get to try a new recipe for banana bread. Or I'll save folding laundry for watching *West Wing* reruns.

Instead of dreading writing days, I now look forward to them because I know I'll get to enjoy a lot of fun stuff between all the writing stuff. And the good news—I'll accomplish something that's important to me.

Remember: You Only Need to Be 40 Percent Brave

My friend Susy made a magnet for me that says, "You Are 40% Brave!" It helps me remember that I don't need to be 100 percent ready— sometimes all I need is 40 percent to get started.

Standing up to the Perfectionism and Procrastination bullies takes bravery. To quit postponing—to look hard, uncomfortable things squarely in the eye and say, "You will not take me down, phone call to my insurance company I don't want to make!"—takes courage, especially when it would be so much easier to just put it at the bottom of my to-do list (or on tomorrow's to-do list).

But you only need a bit of bravery. You don't have to do everything today. You don't have to know exactly how it's going to work out.

You just have to look up the phone number for your insurance company today. You can call them tomorrow.

You just have to organize your bills today. You can pay them tomorrow.

You just have to make your shopping list today. You can go shopping tomorrow.

Just take the very first step.

Now stop. That's enough bravery for today.

That thing you keep putting off—cleaning out the car, getting the toilet repaired, making a phone call to a relative you haven't spoken to in months, making a meal plan—the thing that looks silly to the rest of the world? I get it. Everyone has their own dragon. And my dragon (taking my car in for an oil change) looks silly and slightly puny to you. But trust me, it takes bravery to fight my dragon.

Just as it takes bravery to fight yours.

Have a Bravery Buddy

Sometimes, we need a little social peer pressure to get us out of grooves we've worn into our lives from years of practice. Do you have an understanding friend who can hold you accountable for those things you want to stop putting off? Someone who won't beat you up but will ask how she can cheer you on?

Here are some things you can tell your buddy you need to hear (and some things you can tell your buddy when she needs an extra shot of bravery):

- "I believe in you because I've seen you do other brave things like…"

- "You only have to take the next step. What is the next fifteen-minute step you can take?"
- "I admire you!"
- "You teach me how to be okay even when I'm feeling uncomfortable. Thank you!"

One Rebel's Story

I always assumed my perfectionism affected only me.

That all changed when I noticed my four-year-old trying to make his bed. He tugged angrily at the comforter and then crumpled with his sheets into a heap on his floor. He looked at me—utterly defeated—as I stood in his doorway.

"I can't do it, Mom. I can't do it like you."

He thought his bed had to be perfect, and when he couldn't get it "perfect" like I did, he gave up.

Since then, I have made an intentional effort to battle my perfectionism. Here are three things I have done to help:

1. I say aloud (to him and to myself), "It doesn't have to be perfect."
2. I aim for excellence, not perfection.
3. I allow my children to do things their way instead of forcing them to do things my way. If their beds aren't made perfectly or their rooms aren't cleaned perfectly, it's okay. The important thing is that they tried.

Lindsey Bell

And remember… "Done is better than perfect" (Sheryl Sandberg).

When I start to feel stuck, unworthy, or unqualified, I remember the saying, "Done is better than perfect."

There are a lot of perfect novels sitting in drawers, never finished, never seeing the light of day. There are a lot of perfect shower singers out there who never go out for the community choir. There are a lot of people who would be perfect for jobs but never send in their application.

It's the brave people who send in the less-than-perfect novel to an editor, who sing imperfectly in public, and apply for jobs they are less than perfect for. Brave living is taking the first step—never mind how small—and then, realizing it didn't kill you, being brave enough to take the second step.

What Braver Living Looks Like

My son Justen decided to self-publish a novel. He is an excellent writer, but I (Kathi) knew the trials and tribulations of publishing and wanted to shield him from all of that. So as he shared with me his self-publishing journey, I kept thinking about all the wisdom I'd ever heard from other self-published authors:

- Hire a professional artist to do your book cover.
- Hire a professional editor to edit the book.
- Have a website.
- Take a marketing class.

I suggested all of these things to Justen, but he wasn't interested. I even panicked a little when he told me his friend was editing the book. But my husband reminded me that Justen was moving forward on the book, and I needed to be cheering him on. Anyway, twenty-two-year-olds are not known for taking career advice from their mommies.

We tried to keep expectations low: "Justen, if you sell one hundred copies, that is great. You are a first time author, and that would be amazing." But his goal? A thousand copies.

Gulp.

We are now six months out from Justen's publishing date. His sales? Over thirteen hundred copies and still selling well.

Was it better for him to get it published or make it perfect?

I was squashing the rebel in my son. For his own good, I told myself.

Did he get criticized for having typos in his book? Yes. But the most important part of that sentence? *His.* Justen has a book.

Avoiding criticism isn't a worthy goal. The only way you will avoid criticism is if you stop showing up, stop putting yourself out there. The next time you fear criticism, stop trying so hard to avoid it and ask yourself:

- Am I doing something new? People who are comfortable in never changing their lives are the first to criticize those who do.

- Am I being brave? It takes courage to say, "This is new to me—I don't know everything, but I'm marching forward!"

- Am I doing what God is asking me to do right now?

- Am I doing the best I can, at this very moment, with the resources and knowledge I have right now?

- Am I willing to share my successes and struggles with others around me as I learn?

If the answer is yes—march on, friend!

Right now, I'm stepping into the new world of podcasting. I don't know a lot about it, and it's easy for me to be embarrassed—"I should know how to do this! I wish I was better at this!" But really, I can only be as good as I am today, and maybe tomorrow, by trying something new, I can be a little better. But I'm going to be a whole lotta bad before I can do anything well.

Are you in the midst of something new? If you're being criticized, look at the source. As Brené Brown says, "I only listen to those who are in the ring." Listen to other brave people who are doing their own brave things, not those who are sitting comfortably in the spectator section.

And when you need that extra shot of bravery? Here are a few things that help me be brave when everything in my body tells me, *Stop, don't do it!*

- Go watch TED talks by people who have done brave things.[6]

- Read about the heroes of the Bible.

- Ask people you admire to tell stories about their lives.

- Ask a friend to tell you the bravest thing she remembers doing.

We'll learn how many people refuse to be paralyzed by the bully belief, "If I can't do it right, I won't do it at all," and it's all because they totally reframe it and redefine success as action and obedience, not based on perfect results.

If you are moving forward, imperfectly, know that you are being brave. Each time you make the braver choice, it will be easier, because you will know more, expect the hard work, and also remember the satisfaction that comes with persevering.

Tiny Acts of Rebellion

1. I will post a bad day on Facebook and not just when my cookies turn out Pinterest worthy.

2. I will take a class in something I've always wanted to try, but probably wouldn't be good at (art, writing, pottery).

3. I will show a friend an early draft, a rough sketch, or a baking prototype to get feedback instead of waiting until it's perfect.

4. I will limit my time around media that portrays perfection (including Martha Stewart and certain pages on Pinterest).

5. I will choose to hang out with people who honor the process, not just the product.

Tips for Each Rebel Type

Expressive

Your naturally playful approach to life is a major asset when it comes to this bully belief. "Let's have fun and get it done!" is likely to be your mantra. And in many situations, you can help get and keep the ball rolling for those who are stuck in the paralysis of analysis. As long as you pass off projects that do need to be done perfectly to someone who has that skill set (I hire an accountant to keep me out of jail, for instance), keep making "good enough" a party everyone wants to attend!

Analytic

You know you've fallen into the hands of the Perfectionism bully when you hold your work even after the deadline because it's still not good enough. Dooming yourself to a score of 0 percent when you could have gotten 75 percent is not logical, no matter how much the idea of a *C* grade makes you cringe. Too many Analytic artists die with their music still inside of them because they cannot bring themselves to share their works in progress. Don't settle for nothing; that's the ultimate failure. Give us the best you've got right now.

Driver

You often flip this bully belief into a useful filter: "Whatever I commit to do, I commit to doing well." Your refusal to waste valuable time, energy, or resources on mediocre work is an asset. One liability to watch for, however, is your tendency to overestimate how much you can get done in a certain timeframe. When projects take longer than you planned, you become anxious to move on because, after all, they should be done by now. Practice developing patience by following through all the way to the finish line.

Amiable

Refuse to buy into the common myth that your personality type is lazy. Your God-given assets lead you to take a "slow and steady" pace for most projects. When you find yourself avoiding getting started or taking the next step, ask yourself why. If you're under pressure and feeling stressed, Procrastination may be attempting a hostile takeover. Outside observers may not be able to tell, but check your heart: are you motivated by fear or love? Avoidance is evidence of fear. Taking the next necessary step is the approach of love.

CHAPTER 11

Be a Rebel with a Cause

Good girls get angry, but for all the right reasons.

※

*"Usually when people are sad, they don't do anything.
They just cry over their condition. But when they
get angry, they bring about a change."*

JAMES RUSSELL LOWELL[7]

Bully belief 3: "I don't do angry."

I (Kathi) didn't think I should write this chapter. I don't consider myself an angry person. I don't throw fits in the middle of Target when they run out of sale-priced grapes, I rarely yell (unless my dog takes off into the middle of oncoming traffic), and I don't tend to leave dents in other people's cars (even when I know they deserve them).

All my life I've been told that anger is a bad emotion. Girls who got angry were sent to the principal's office, and in my third-grade mind, there was no worse place on the planet than the principal's office.

So I learned a variety of ways to keep my anger in check. When someone called me a name (which, when you're a chubby red-headed girl with freckles and a Dorothy Hamill haircut, happened regularly), instead of letting my anger show, I would use a variety of techniques to hide it:

- digging a pencil into my thigh to get my mind off the anger
- making snide comments about the person teasing me (in third grade, these usually included the witty and urbane "poop head")
- biting the inside of my cheeks until they bled

That last one was the least helpful of all since as soon as I did that, my brother would bite the inside of his cheeks to mock me. There may or may not have been some punching after some of those incidents.

Like I said, I'm not a yeller. Oh, that doesn't mean I don't have anger issues, it just means you should usually be more worried if I'm quiet than if I'm raising my voice.

That is until Father's Day.

June had been crazy. In a ten-day period, I was home for only one day—Father's Day, and I was going to make it great for my man, Roger. First Roger, my daughter Kimberly, and I were going to Starbucks, and then across town to Sunny Donuts to get Roger's favorite donut, the angel cream. Then we had a BBQ dinner planned with the whole family, and some time curled up on the couch, just Roger and me, before I had to do laundry and pack up to be back on the road the next day. It was going to be a crazy day, but a great day.

Roger, Kimberly, and I drove to Starbucks, happy and chatty and looking forward to our mini food road trip. And that's when "The Starbucks Incident" happened.

While we were waiting our turn to merge into the main drive-thru lane, a Mercedes-Benz with two women in it drove in from the other lane and cut in front of our car. I could not believe what happened. I was stunned. Our car erupted with reactions:

- Roger honked the horn (we have been married over eight years and he has never, I mean never, honked his horn before).

- Kimberly kept repeating, "Oh no they didn't! Oh no they didn't!"

- I rolled down my window and screamed, "Are you *kidding* me! Who raised you?"

I thought I'd recovered sufficiently, but then Roger said, "Kathi, I need you to calm down."

Through gritted teeth, I growled back at him, "I am calm!"

"So why are you unbuckling your seatbelt?"

Okay—maybe I wasn't as calm as I thought.

I wanted them to know they couldn't hide from me. I took out my phone and took a picture of the back of their car. What I thought I was going to do with that picture—post it on signs around the neighborhood or on Twitter?—I didn't know. I just needed them to know, "I saw what you did." (As if the yelling wasn't enough of a clue.)

We continued to seethe for the rest of our time in line. I was so angry (and I thought justifiably so), but there wasn't anything I could do about it except grumble and complain.

When we finally arrived at the Starbucks window and the other car had driven away, the young barista looked a bit confused. He handed us our tray of drinks and said, "I don't really understand what's happening, but that car ahead of you bought all your drinks and told me to tell you that they were raised by wolves."

We All Do Angry

Anger happens to us all, and sometimes it's for a good reason. We see an injustice being committed, we've been cheated by someone, someone is mistreating another person or an animal—these are all justifiable reasons to be angry.

And then there are the "justifiable" reasons for anger: You didn't get the raise you'd hoped for from the boss for whom you've sacrificed time away from your family. Your kids are openly disobeying you and your husband. Your husband made a promise to you and didn't keep it. The anger can look like anything from mild irritation to a simmering rage that is hard to contain, but it is still there.

Our problem comes when we start to believe the lie that anger is inherently a bad thing. Anger isn't a bad thing. Unprocessed anger is a bad thing.

We are all going to experience anger. Most of us avoid dealing with it in one way or another, and that's where we get into trouble.

What kind of anger avoider are you? For each question, circle the response(s) that you would do or would love to do:

1. It's 10:00 p.m., and my husband has not acknowledged my birthday.
    My reaction is to
    a) tell myself that he's just forgotten…and it's no big deal anyway.
    b) resent all time and effort I've put into the great birthday parties I've
        thrown for him and gifts I've given him.
    c) say, with forced cheerfulness, "It was so nice of your mother to call
        to wish me a happy birthday today!"
    d) let my anger finally spill out via tears and accusations.

2. I'm trying to make a simple return, but the customer service agent acts
    like it's a huge imposition. When she says, "Well, I'm not even sure we
    can take this back." My response is to
    a) smile and wait pleasantly for her to figure it out, keeping my
        thoughts to myself.
    b) write a letter of complaint later that evening, once I realize how
        mad she really made me.
    c) sigh, pull out my cell phone, and start texting while I wait for her
        to figure it all out.
    d) say "Well, I'm sure you *can!*" in a loud and determined voice.

3. I've brought my car in to have all four tires replaced, which I was told
    would take one-and-a-half to two hours. It's been four hours, and my
    car is still not ready. I
    a) try to keep myself calm by watching mindless TV in the waiting
        room.
    b) work myself into a migraine fretting about the inconvenience and
        waste of time.
    c) ask "Is it done yet?" every fifteen minutes and complain loudly to
        friends via cell phone.
    d) demand to talk to the manager and tell him that I'm going to give
        them a low Yelp rating for such inexcusably poor service.

4. When someone changes lanes suddenly, causing me to swerve and
    brake, I react by
    a) shaking my head and sighing because some people just don't know
        how to drive.

b) turning the incident into an "ain't it awful" story that I tell every one for the rest of the day.

c) getting in front of him and then driving slowly to make sure he gets a taste of his own medicine.

d) yelling, "Where'd you get your driver's license? Correspondence school?"

5. While out to dinner, I order my favorite dish without onions. It looks fine when the server brings it to me, but when I take my first bite I can tell it's full of onions. I

a) say nothing and choke it down; I don't want to make a scene.

b) spend ten minutes telling my companion how this kind of thing always happens to me; no matter where I go, nobody ever gets it right.

c) sarcastically comment to my server that he must be new and still learning how to take down orders correctly.

d) angrily flag down my server and loudly proclaim, "I said *no onions!*"

6. When I've warned my daughter about the consequences of a choice, but she goes ahead and does it anyway, I'm likely to

a) shift my anger (she didn't listen to me) into guilt (a good parent would have gotten through).

b) call all my friends and vent about how upset I am, but say nothing directly to my daughter.

c) say, "Well, I hate to say 'I told you so,' but…"

d) tell her in no uncertain terms how immature I think she is.

7. I've spent all day cleaning the house when I find muddy boot tracks from the backyard, through the kitchen, and up the stairs. When I find the culprit, I

a) ask him to pay closer attention next time.

b) mop up the mess, all the while rehearsing all the ways my family takes me for granted.

c) say, "Well, it's nice that someone gets to do what she wants around here."

d) go into Drama Mama mode, starting with "After all I do around here…"

8. During a job performance review, my boss levels an unfair critique at me. I immediately
   a) put on my poker face so he cannot tell how upset I'm feeling.
   b) plan to tell all my coworkers what a jerk he is.
   c) start thinking of passive-aggressive ways to get him back.
   d) snap, "That's not right!"

9. The neighbor's dog has been barking for hours. This happens all the time. This time, I
   a) once again reach for earplugs and wish I had better neighbors.
   b) post a Facebook update about barking dogs and selfish neighbors.
   c) give my neighbors the cold shoulder the next time I see them.
   d) finally call and give my neighbors a piece of my mind.

10. When I feel like God hasn't shown up like I expected him to, my natural response is to
   a) swallow my disappointment and try to move on. After all, who am I to question God?
   b) spend the next women's Bible study discussion time chronicling all the times God's let me down.
   c) throw myself all the more into doing godly deeds; at least I can be counted on to come through.
   d) rant directly to him, demanding to know, "Why?"

Now record below the number of times you circled each letter. This will help you identify how you most often deal with anger.

a = Stuffer
b = Stewer
c = Seeper
d = Screamer

The Stuffer

"I'm fine," is the mantra of the stuffer. "Don't worry about me. I'll be fine." The stuffer would rather deal with her anger by not dealing with it at all.

And some of us are situational stuffers. We've all heard of celebrities who have a sweet-as-pie persona when it comes to press tours and *Entertainment Tonight* interviews. They let everything roll off their back in public, but then it comes out later that they are impossible to work with, rage against the crew on movie sets, or belittle their assistants for ordering the wrong latte.

But you don't have to be a celebrity to be a situational stuffer. Maybe everyone in your office thinks you are one of those rare people who just doesn't have a temper. You seemingly let everything roll off your back without ever fighting back.

The problem with not dealing with anger is that it's going to come out one way or another—and probably not at the time you would like it to. Your boss yelled at you, but instead of dealing with it, you go home and ignore your husband and kids.

In an episode of *How I Met Your Mother* titled "The Chain of Screaming," Marshall is afraid of being yelled at by his boss, nicknamed Artillery Arthur, when the report he is supposed to turn in is not finished. Every one of Marshall's friends tells him how they would explain the unfinished report to Arthur, but Barney tells Marshall he should just yell at one of his subordinates to release his frustration. The way "The Chain of Screaming" works is that you scream at someone "below" you, then that person screams at another person, and so on down the line.

Barney is encouraging Marshall to stuff his feelings about his boss. But even Barney is smart enough to know that those feelings are going to come out somewhere, even if it's totally unrelated to the real reason for the anger.

And that's what happens to the stuffer—stuffing doesn't work forever. It's going to lead to something else. One day you're going to be waiting for your number to be called at the bakery, and when the counter clerk skips over your number, you're gonna lose your mind. There may be yelling, an insistence to talk to her manager, or snarkiness directed at her when you finally do get waited on. All because you stuffed your anger over your child getting home an hour after curfew.

I can tend toward stuffing tendencies, especially around people I love dearly. I don't want to deal, so I stuff. But you can keep that beach ball underwater only for so long. Eventually, it's going to pop up to the surface.

The Stewer

This is the woe-is-me type of anger that comes up every time a stewer is with another person. Everyone she talks to is subjected to the long list of injustices that have been done to her. She is hard to be around because her favorite topic of conversation is how miserable her life is. At first, it can feel great to be on this person's side—you hear what everyone else in the family/office/church is doing wrong. Until you realize your list of transgressions is being repeated to everyone else she knows as well.

Often a stewer loves rules and regulations and lives to keep track of how everyone else is doing it wrong. Think of Dwight of *The Office*—he can remember everyone that's ever done him wrong.

The stewer will never, I mean never, let it go. When you've moved on, she is still stuck in the event that happened six years ago that you can't even remember.

And the problem with never letting it go? They keep adding perceived injury to perceived slight and insult, throw in some unreturned phone calls and a late birthday card and you have a bitterness stew that no one can swallow.

If you are a stewer, you may lean toward overanalysis of every situation, action, and reaction. Stewers tend to assign the worst motives to people.

A friend who is a stewer invited me to a gathering at her house. The only problem? I didn't know it. She had mistyped my email address into the invite and the error message hit her spam filter. She didn't talk to me for weeks because she thought I'd snubbed her. I learned from another friend why I was suddenly in the doghouse. If only she'd come to me and said why she was frustrated, we could have cleared it up. But I get the feeling she's still a little ticked at me for missing her party—the party I never knew was happening.

The Seeper

The seeper is mad, and she's going to let you know it in the calmest way possible. She is the one who will remind you that "if you'd only listen to me, your life could be so much better." The seeper's need for control makes her angry every time someone goes against her. I think of

Raymond's mom, Marie Barone, on *Everyone Loves Raymond*. Every dig at Deborah, Raymond's wife, about her cooking, housekeeping, and parenting is served up with a smile and a big side dish of condescension. Here are the tools of the seeper:

- sighs

- eye rolls

- back-handed compliments ("It's amazing you're even able to warm up a frozen dinner with how little time you get to spend at home with your kids.")

- offers to help because you're doing it wrong

This comes out in Facebook posts all the time. Just today, I posted about getting back to the gym after a long absence. (Stop judging.) Immediately, someone posted, "Oh, you shouldn't be going to that gym, you should go to mine. You'll burn more calories in a shorter amount of time." I know this person, so the next time I post about my frustrations about not losing weight, they will come back with "I told you, you should have gone to my gym."

The seeper is "just trying to help," but the help always comes with a side of anger and judgment. Seepers want to help, but only if it's on their terms.

The Screamer

Think Ricky Ricardo in *I Love Lucy*. The screamer is the person you tiptoe around so that she has no reason to blow her cool.

It's hard to be around a screamer, but it's hard being one as well. There is no room to process emotions, no room to take anyone else into consideration, and no way to get to a place of peace—it's 0 to 60 in every circumstance.

All four of these reactions to anger lead only to deeper issues, one of the biggest being bitterness. Anger that is unresolved and left to fester will eventually lead to a deep bitterness that will affect not only our emotional lives, but our mental, spiritual, and physical lives as well.

One Rebel's Story

A few years ago, I began walking a path I never imagined having to take: the path of baby loss. I lost four babies to miscarriage. After my first loss, I cried a lot.

What I didn't do was allow myself to feel anger.

Anytime anger began to surface, I stuffed it deep inside the cavities of my heart. I mistakenly assumed it was wrong to be mad, that it was wrong to question how a God of love could allow something like this into the life of his child. Anytime I felt anger toward him, I forced myself to pretend everything was okay.

This worked (or at least seemed to work) up until we lost a second baby. Those emotions I had been stuffing resurfaced in depression. I wasn't able to enjoy the children I had because I obsessed on the children I had lost…and on the God who allowed me to lose them.

It was only after months of counseling that I finally learned to stop stuffing my anger. God is big enough to handle our emotions, and he'll help us work through them once we allow ourselves to really feel them.

Lindsey Bell

It's Okay to Get Angry

"'In your anger do not sin': Do not let the sun go down while you are still angry, and do not give the devil a foothold" (Ephesians 4:26-27).

Anger is not a sin. How you handle it can be done in either a sinful or a godly way.

When your body is in pain, it's a signal that something is wrong that needs to be righted. It's the same with anger. Anger is a signal that something is wrong in your world. It is neither good nor bad; it just is.

It's what we do with that anger that can lead to sin. In the passage from Ephesians, we are told not only that anger isn't a sin, but also what to do with it.

In your anger do not sin. Anger is okay—throwing chairs is not. This is the *blowing up* part of anger. (See the Screamer and the Seeper above.)

When our anger comes out in unhealthy ways, either by putting some-one down or intimidating someone verbally or physically, this is sinning in anger. Not only does it affect the people around you, but it eats you up inside as well. It may be expressed, but at what cost?

"Do not let the sun go down while you are still angry." While sinning in anger is the *blowing up* part of the verse, the sun going down on your anger is the *stuffing down* part. (See the Stuffer and the Stewer above.)

"Do not give the devil a foothold." Any of these ways of dealing (or not dealing) with our anger causes us to distance ourselves from others and from God.

How to Handle Our Anger

First, we must recognize that there are situations that we must stay angry about. When my son, Justen, was being bullied in elementary school, the pastor over the school said to me, "Is that really the worst thing in your life? Then count yourself lucky." (This was before the days of bully awareness.) I was angry and needed to stay that way until the situation was resolved. (We finally changed schools to get away from the situation.) When we see injustice, bullying, mistreatment, or corrup-tion, God has given us the tool of anger to keep us focused on the issue. Anger, in the right situation and used correctly, can change us and oth-ers for the better.

Of course, there are those situations where our anger, while it may be justifiable, is a waste and needs to be dealt with—not with the per-son or situation, but between us and God.

Roger and I live in a townhouse community. We are the rare Califor-nians who not only know everyone on our side of the block, but we like them all. We are blessed with neighbors who bring over dinner when someone's sick, check up on each other when something looks funny at someone's house, and generally are a part of one another's lives.

I love where I live, with one exception: our neighbors on the next block. I'm not really sure who all lives in this house. What I do know is that they spend an inordinate amount of their time and energy taking up as many parking spaces on our street as possible. This family parks their five cars, one in front of each other, spaced exactly one and a half cars apart, thus taking up two extra spaces on our busy street. This way, on special occasions, they can have their guests park near their house.

Recently, as Roger and I were passing by their cars, I told him, "I fantasize about leaving passive-aggressive notes on their car or depositing Jake's (our dog's) poop bags on their doorstep."

"Well, fortunately, you are too evolved for that," Roger said.

Isn't that sweet—he thinks I'm a good person and not just terrified of getting caught.

And as silly as this situation is, it's amazing how much mental, spiritual, and emotional energy being mad about it drains from me. I have no power to change the situation. Our homeowners' board has tried. Legally, there is nothing to be done. And my anger isn't selfish—my family and guests would rarely park at that end of the street.

Is it an injustice? Somewhat. While they aren't breaking any city laws, they are selfish and downright unneighborly. And it's easy to steam about it every time I walk my dog past their home. But almost every day I have to remind myself, *the only one affected by my anger is me.* They don't even know that I'm angry. I can't change the situation. The only thing I can change is my reaction to the situation.

And that's the key—knowing when anger is going to serve the situation as well as knowing when anger is only going to hurt you and those you love.

Yes, anger is a tool that can often right injustices and serve others when it is acted on appropriately. But it helps to know when anger is appropriate. I love this little quiz from Duke University on when to stay angry and when to deal with your emotions in a different way:

> There are even ways to improve your ability to cope with stress, according to Dr. Redford Williams, director of Duke University's Behavioral Medicine Research Center. "When something distresses you ask yourself these four questions: 'Is this important?' If the answer's 'yes' then ask, 'Is my reaction reasonable?' If so ask, 'Is the situation modifiable?' and if so ask yourself, 'Would it be worth making the effort to change the situation?'" Williams explained. "A 'no' to any of these questions means you need to chill out."[8]

However, four *yes* answers means you need to take action and assert yourself in a way that is appropriate to the situation.

But what we are feeling on the inside doesn't justify bad behavior on the outside. "Anger is part of being human," says Norman Rosenthal, MD, professor of psychiatry at Georgetown University Medical School. "Problems start when you bottle it up, react now and think later, or feel that a destructive response is justified just because you're furious."[9]

I guess I'll have to rise above the passive-aggressive notes and blue bags on the front step.

Do a Reality Check

Yesterday I ran into Starbucks to grab a few gift cards and drinks for Roger and me while he was at a doctor's appointment. I figured I would be in and out of there in five minutes. What I failed to consider was that it was December 23 and everyone in Los Gatos, California, had decided at that exact moment to run into this particular Starbucks and get a drink and a gift card.

I looked at the line and decided I would probably be there for twenty minutes. At that point, I had to make a decision whether it was worth being late picking up Roger to get the drinks and cards. Since two of the gift cards were for employees at the doctor's office where Roger was, I decided to text him to let him know I would be late.

After getting to the front of the line and getting my purchase rung up, another woman came up right behind me and started to yell at the people behind me in line, "I just need a gift card! I can't wait in this line!" And as people started to weigh in on her rudeness, she turned a deaf ear. Finally, one of the baristas assured this woman that a lot of people were there just to get gift cards and that it took just as long to ring up a gift card as it did to order a drink.

One of the best ways to diffuse anger in yourself is to do a reality check. Instead of stewing in line or cutting in front of other people, look at the situation and see how you can make it work for you. After thinking through the different outcomes, I decided, yes, I will wait in this twenty-minute line because that will save me from having to come back later, wait in line, and make another trip to the doctor's office to drop off the gifts. I also let the other person affected by my decision know what was going on and got his buy in so that I wasn't making anyone else crazy.

Assume the Best in People

This can be hard to do in the heat of the moment, but it's worth it to try. Yesterday I got in the checkout line at the grocery store just as another woman got out of line and went to the next aisle. After a few minutes of her line not moving, she decided she wanted back in my line—in front of me.

And I seethed. When I tried to talk to her about it, it was obvious that English was not her native language. So I had to make some quick decisions.

- I didn't want to get the store involved.

- I had to admit that I was frustrated that not everyone was following the rules.

- I also had to admit that this woman may not have known what she was doing.

So I decided to let it go. I didn't just accept it and skip on my merry way, however. I had a process to let it go.

1. *I admitted I may not have all the facts.* Maybe she was confused. Maybe not. I didn't know. My son sometimes gets irritated with me for being gullible, but it's not that I'm naïve. It's that finally, after several decades on this planet, I understand that I may not know everything in a situation, and it's not worth it to lose my mind.

2. *I admitted that I was frustrated.* Instead of trying to pretend that it didn't bother me, I admitted to myself that it did bother me. If she had taken my wallet, I would have acted, but since it was just my place in line, I made the decision to be frustrated for a moment, and then let it go.

3. *I admitted my anger to a friend.* I texted my husband, who validated me but also told me he was proud of the way I handled it. I've come to realize if I can just have one person to affirm me, it can make me feel validated.

Now maybe you would have made a different decision. That's OK. We all have to make the best decision for ourselves. Maybe my friend would have called over the manager, and that would have been the right decision for her.

When we're bitter, everything and everyone bugs us. Bitterness is like a termite infestation that gnaws away at us. We look fine on the outside, but we're disintegrating on the inside. Anger that leads to bitterness causes real destruction in our lives. But when we stop trying harder to avoid our anger and start living braver, we get to experience and then resolve our anger and live our lives free from bitterness.

Tiny Acts of Rebellion

1. When I'm frustrated when my kids don't do their chores, I will let them know in a calm, direct manner instead of stewing, screaming, stuffing, or seeping.

2. I will bravely discuss an issue I've been having with a friend with care and grace.

3. I will allow myself to get angry when I see an injustice taking place and will act on my anger.

4. I will prayerfully seek God when my anger is out of control.

Tips for Each Rebel Type

Expressive

You usually manage your anger by dressing it up in cuteness and humor. But when something you've been eagerly anticipating doesn't happen or doesn't turn out the way you'd expected, you can become really upset. Since you don't express your big negative emotions very often, trying to keep your happy face most of the time, people are often surprised and even shocked by how far down you can go. As you learn to honestly express your anger and other big emotions, your highs will still be high and far less forced, while your lows won't be as low.

Analytic

You tend to express anger as pain and disappointment. If one of your children lets you down, for example, rather than saying, "You let me

down," you might say, "I must be a terrible mother for you to have…"
Of all the personalities, you're the most likely to physicalize negative
emotions as headaches, stomachaches, and so on. While your sensitivity to others is an asset, it becomes a liability when you use it as a reason
not to be honest with others about your big emotions.

Driver

You're likely to think, *Oh, I do angry. Just watch me!* The fact that you
rarely let anyone walk all over you is an asset. But brutal honesty, especially at the wrong time and place, can be a huge liability. Often, you
aren't aware of how others perceive you. You may intimidate and even
scare the people closest to you. The best way to find out is to ask and be
receptive to honest input at a time when emotions are not running high.
Develop agreements and signals to protect your relationships when anger
and other negative emotions flare.

Amiable

Since your idea of victory is peace—often at any cost—anger and
other negative emotions appear to be major threats to your well-being.
Keep in mind that emotions are not positive or negative; they are simply signals. It's what you do with them that determines whether they're
productive or destructive. If you try to suppress all emotions you consider negative, you will simultaneously stunt your ability to feel and
express positive emotions. As you learn to honestly experience and process all emotions, anger will become less terrifying, and you will be able
to restore your equilibrium much faster.

CHAPTER 12

This Probably Isn't the End of the World

How to pick battles worthy of your time and energy.

✳

*"But feelings can't be ignored, no matter how
unjust or ungrateful they seem."*

ANNE FRANK, *The Diary of a Young Girl*

> **Bully belief 4:** "Everything I feel is valid and must be valued."

I (Cheri) am not the kind of person who has to be right.

I married someone like that. I married Mr. Right—and then found out his first name was Always. Turns out we're the perfect couple: He has to be right. And I hate being wrong. I will go to great lengths to avoid being wrong, prove why I wasn't wrong, and show why you're wrong for saying I'm wrong.

I hate being wrong. When someone implies that I'm wrong, I get upset. And when I get upset, this totally unfair condition takes over my mind. It's called "losing it." When I get upset, I lose my mind.

Here's just one example: I'm in junior high and John, my only sibling, is in college. We are playing *Monopoly* together, and I am losing. Only this day is different from all the other times we've played *Monopoly*. This time, I decide to read the rules.

I find out, for the first time in my life, that there is no rule stating that the oldest player is always the banker. Nor do the rules say anything about the banker earning a $500 salary every time he passes *Go*.

My entire childhood has been a lie. My big brother has been cheating all along! Worse, he just gives me that condescending, "How could you be so gullible?" look.

I lose it, right then and there, at the expensive corner with Park Place and Boardwalk. I throw my B&O Railroad card at him and give him a piece of my mind.

"You are the worst…" I begin in a fury. Oh, how I want to hurl the perfect insult. And I have hundreds, even thousands, of possible options to finish my sentence. But remember what happens to me when I get upset?

Sure enough, my poor lost mind makes the lamest possible choice: "You are the worst brother I have!"

And if there's anything that makes me more upset than being wrong, it's being laughed at by the worst (and only) brother I have while I'm in the midst of being so very wrong.

I'm not proud to admit it, but this was no one-time incident. I have a track record of "losing it." In every area of life. Regularly. Each time I lost it, I promised myself it would be the last. And each time I couldn't keep that promise, the bullies heaped on the guilt and shame.

"How can you call yourself a Christian when you keep losing it like this?"

"Anyone who loses it as often as you do is nothing but a loser."

Are You a Loser?

If you frequently hear, "You are the most emotionally healthy person I know," you may not find this chapter particularly practical. (Although reading it may help you better understand those in your life who live on the emotionally intense end of the spectrum.) But if you're a sister screamer, seeper, stuffer, or stewer, read on!

Directions: For each question, circle *Yes* or *No*. Leave the blank empty for now.

_____	1.	Yes No	All my life I've been told, "You're too sensitive."
_____	2.	Yes No	I expect others to validate my feelings.
_____	3.	Yes No	I hate unresolved conflicts and will pursue people to make sure we've achieved closure.
_____	4.	Yes No	I believe in venting my emotions to get them all out in the open.
_____	5.	Yes No	I have a hard time experiencing opposing emotions simultaneously, such as sadness and gratitude or anger and curiosity.

_____ 6. Yes No   I tend to keep explaining my feelings until I believe the other person has understood me.

_____ 7. Yes No   I tend to blame my feelings on others, saying or thinking that they "made me mad" (or whatever the emotion may be).

_____ 8. Yes No   A certain amount of complaining is normal and healthy.

_____ 9. Yes No   Some of my emotions are so intense, I'm afraid of them.

_____ 10. Yes No   I wish I could just avoid certain emotions.

_____ 11. Yes No   I keep a gratitude list.

_____ 12. Yes No   I have several strategies for responding to unexpected emotions.

_____ 13. Yes No   I have safe people in my life who can help me deal with my emotions when they become overwhelming.

_____ 14. Yes No   People sometimes feel that they have to walk on eggshells around me.

_____ 15. Yes No   I am ashamed of being so emotional.

_____ 16. Yes No   Some people are just naturally critical.

_____ 17. Yes No   I am proud of being so emotional.

_____ 18. Yes No   My emotional nature comes with specific strengths, such as empathy.

_____ 19. Yes No   I often wish I could find the off switch for my emotions (or better yet, pull the plug on them altogether).

_____ 20. Yes No   I'm in at least one relationship in which I'm waiting for the other person to change how they react to me before I change how I treat them.

_____ 21. Yes No   People close to me aren't completely honest with me because they don't want to risk a big emotional reaction.

_____ 22. Yes No   When I'm angry or upset with someone, it's hard or impossible for me to treat them with kindness and respect until my anger is resolved.

_____ 23. Yes No   I often replay difficult conversations in my mind; I
                        can still hear the negative tones of voice and see the
                        upset facial expressions.

_____ 24. Yes No   I sometimes get stuck waiting for someone to vali-
                        date, understand, hear, or apologize to me.

_____ 25. Yes No   I've been called an "attention seeker" or "drama
                        queen" or "control freak," especially by people who
                        don't understand me.

_____ Total

Write in the following point values in the blank in front of each statement and total up your score. For example, if you circled Yes for statement 16, 18, or 23, write a 1 in the blank next to it. If you circled Yes for
statement 8, 10, 11, and so on, write a 2 next to it.

1 point: 16 Yes; 18 Yes; 23 Yes

2 points: 8 Yes; 10 Yes; 11 No; 12 No; 13 No; 14 No; 15 Yes; 17 Yes;
    19 Yes; 20 Yes; 21 Yes

3 points: 1 Yes; 2 Yes; 3 Yes; 4 Yes; 5 Yes; 6 Yes; 7 Yes; 9 Yes; 22 Yes;
    24 Yes; 25 Yes

If your score is 20 or lower, "losing it" probably is not a frequent
    issue for you.

If your score is 21-40, "losing it" is a problem you'll want to deal with
    before it escalates.

If your score is 41+, your tendency to "lose it" is probably causing
    your physical health and the health of your relationships to suffer.

One Rebel's Story, Part 1

I should have known it was coming.

That morning we have to get out the door, so I assign
tasks. They do their usual—start and get sidetracked. So I
do my usual—feel irritated I have to waste more words on
stupid reminders.

I just want to get them out the door with shoes on. Okay,
with shoes and coats and gloves and hats and backpacks and
snacks and waters (times four).

Our resident grumbler complains about my snack choice. I sweetly remind him he *does* like pretzels and applesauce, and if he wants a snack today, this is it. He returns thirty seconds later with a granola bar. "Can't I just take this for snack?"

I semi-sweetly tell him no and get back to the shoes I told you to put on. But he believes if he asks enough times, he'll eventually wear me down.

And he does. Weeks of kids complaining have added up to this moment. I tell him with an eye roll that I've had enough of his complaints to last me forever.

After only seventeen minor setbacks, we are almost all in the car. Then I hear a child spewing unkind words to another because *no good reason*.

Now I think in all caps, in long, run-on sentences.

WHAT IN THE WORLD, HOW MANY TIMES DO I HAVE TO SPEND MY TIME DEALING WITH ALL THIS GARBAGE? I'M WORKING MY REAR END OFF FOR THEM, AND ALL THEY CAN DO IS WHINE AND COMPLAIN AND FIGHT AND...

Swallowed irritations spew out. I speak harshly. I show them how to react in anger, how to make it all about yourself, how to preach grace one day and throw it out the window the next. What a mess.

After I apologize and after I admit I just taught them things I don't believe, I wonder how to end this cycle of mine.

Angie Parlin

You and Your Big Emotions

Our emotions serve as indicators. What we do with them determines whether their helpful or destructive qualities take the lead. Unfortunately, for many of us, our emotions are like tantrum-throwing toddlers. They often destroy the peace, demand attention, and hold us (and others) hostage.

Out-of-control emotions are evidence of young places in your heart. They need a tender loving touch. I've learned to view these immature places in my heart the way I'd look at a frightened, wounded little girl who is relying on me for help.

The best way I can help her is to take her to Jesus.

"Let the Little Children Come to Me"

How does Jesus respond to the little girl I bring to him? Mark 10:13-16 paints a poignant picture:

> People were bringing little children to Jesus for him to place his hands on them, but the disciples rebuked them. When Jesus saw this, he was indignant. He said to them, "Let the little children come to me, and do not hinder them, for the kingdom of God belongs to such as these. Truly I tell you, anyone who will not receive the kingdom of God like a little child will never enter it." And he took the children in his arms, placed his hands on them and blessed them.

As you imagine this scene, notice two things.

1. Jesus is indignant with anyone who tries to keep the little girl away from him.

So if you feel hesitant, don't believe the voices that say, "He doesn't have time for you!" or "This isn't his problem, it's yours." Instead, hear Jesus's voice, loud and clear, encouraging, "Let the little children come to me, and do not hinder them."

The little girl yearns to be loved; don't hinder her. Take her to Jesus.

2. Jesus declares, "Anyone who will not receive the kingdom of God like a little child will never enter it."

Do you know what he means? How does someone "receive the kingdom of God like a little child"? Keep watching!

Jesus picks the little girl up in his arms.

That's it.

What did she have to do in order to receive Jesus's blessing? She let him pick her up. That's all. He does the rest. He does the heavy lifting, the laying on of hands, and the blessing.

She doesn't have to Try Harder or act better. She doesn't have to promise or prove anything. What she does is the hardest thing for most of us: nothing.

There are some important things she doesn't do. She doesn't refuse, kick, scream, jump down, or run away. All she does is cooperate, surrendering her fears to Jesus's loving embrace.

The same is true for me and you.

How to Stop the Upset Cycle

I love Psalm 18:16, where David shares his own experience of God taking him in his arms:

> He reached down from on high and took hold of me;
> he drew me up out of deep waters.

Big emotions are a lot like the ocean. If you don't know how to approach waves, you can get bowled over by a big one at the beach. Likewise, you can feel blindsided by a tsunami of feelings. If you don't know how to swim in choppy water or cope with ever-changing emotions, you may feel like you're drowning. And if you hold on to heavy weights, you'll end up going under.

1. Practice a New Approach to Waves of Emotion

When I was a child, my father taught me how to get to the calm part of the ocean just beyond the breaking waves: wait for a big wave, and right as it crested, dive into its base. It seemed so counterintuitive. Dive *into* the wave? I was trying to avoid the waves!

As I faced an oncoming wave for the very first time, I fought the urge to *run*. But at the last possible second, as the wave arched over me, I dove into the base and popped up on the other side of the breakers. It worked! For the rest of the day, I practiced my new skill until I could swagger up to any wave with a "you're not the boss of me" attitude. My fear of ocean waves vanished that day because I had a strategy for dealing with them.

You can't control emotion waves any more than you can control ocean waves. They often show up out of nowhere, ready to plow you over. What you need is a strategy, one that you can practice until your fear turns to confidence.

When something upsetting happens, you'll experience a fight-flight-or-freeze signal, a quick jolt of adrenaline triggered by your brain. You have no control over being put suddenly on high alert. However, what you do next will determine whether you're sent spinning wildly out of emotional control or whether you get to handle the situation on your own terms.

If you disengage, everything will return to normal in about thirty minutes. However, if you engage by tensing your body, thinking anxious thoughts, and saying upset words, your body will respond by releasing yet another flood of adrenaline.

Can you see what an exhausting, self-perpetuating cycle this is? The more you react, the more you *react*. In order for you to halt your body's high-alert reactions, you must intentionally stop reacting and start being *response*-able.

Let's rewind back to the initial high-alert warning and try something different.

First, interrupt your thoughts with a simple phrase like "You're okay" as reassurance that extreme emotion is not necessary.

Second, control your breathing. Take a slow, deep breath; hold it for a few seconds, and then exhale slowly. This counters the automatic reflex of inhaling sharply when surprised, which your body reads as alarm.

Third, open your eyes. Intentionally widen your eyes and look around slowly. This is the opposite of your body's reflex of narrowing the field of vision when stressed, which triggers fight, flee, or freeze.

Fourth, reach for an ANCHOR verse to replace the upset thoughts racing through your mind and words coming out of your mouth (see below).

Finally, laugh (if it's possible or appropriate) or exhale deeply. This counteracts the natural stress reflex of holding your breath, which your body will respond to with adrenaline.

2. Hold Fast to ANCHOR Scriptures

While you can't stop the emotional rip currents themselves, you can resist being dragged into the depths of the emotion ocean by setting your mind on God's Word. Develop a collection of specific grounding

ANCHOR verses that you memorize or carry with you. ANCHOR verses do one or more of the following:

Attach to an event. When I was in junior high, my BFF decided she hated me. Ever since then, I've felt insecure about female friendships. When I'm going to be mingling with women I don't know well, I hold onto John 15:16, "You did not choose me, but I chose you."

Name the feeling. The problem with overwhelming anxiety is that it's not an actual emotion. It's a self-perpetuating physiological state. Verses like Psalm 34:4-5 help me recognize the actual emotions I'm feeling so I can work through them.

> I sought the LORD, and he answered me;
>   he delivered me from all my fears.
> Those who look to him are radiant;
>   their faces are never covered with shame.

Create space. When I'm feeling blindsided by a wave of emotion, it's easy to hide in a corner, certain my world is coming to an end. Psalm 18:19 reminds me that

> [God] brought me out into a spacious place;
>   he rescued me because he delighted in me.

This perspective shift helps me get a bigger picture of the problem.

Highlight the real problem. The current problem is rarely the real problem. My husband's comment or a child's messy room doesn't "cause" me to feel overwhelmed. The real problem is my own disconnection from God. Psalm 46:1,10 says,

> God is our refuge and strength
>   an ever-present help in trouble...
> "Be still, and know that I am God."

Both are sequential: Refuge, *then* strength. Be still, *then* know. These verses refocus me on reconnecting with God.

Open your heart. Once I open my heart to hear God's guidance in that moment, I become ready to change my own attitudes and actions, regardless of what others do (or don't) do. "I have loved you with an everlasting love; I have drawn you with unfailing kindness" (Jeremiah 31:3) helps me return to God's love.

Redefine the moment. I used to believe in defining moments. "That awful day when…That terrible moment I heard…" Now I believe in "defining a moment" by prayerfully revisiting a painful past event and putting the old story I've been retelling myself in perspective. Second Corinthians 10:5 says, "we take captive every thought to make it obedient to Christ," which makes it clear that moments don't define me. Only God does.

3. Lighten Your "Baditude" Backpack

I used to think that venting my emotions was helpful. Let it all out. Use friends and family as sounding boards for my frustration. I now see each negative word I speak as a one-pound weight I'm adding to my own backpack even as I'm attempting to tread water.

I've taken the Complaint-Free Challenge every January for the last eight years. The goal is to go the entire month without complaining, criticizing, or gossiping. I wear a bracelet that I switch each time I catch myself in the act.

Each year, I am reminded that the more I complain, criticize, and gossip—aloud or internally—the more quickly I succumb to overwhelming emotions, become upset, and lose my mind. It's not a coincidence; there's a direct correlation.

And since I can't control the outside events that trigger an initial flood of emotion, it's vital that I control what I can: the words I speak aloud and think inside my head.

The "how to" for this is simple: replace "baditude" with gratitude. Notice, I said simple, not easy. It's been eight years, and I'm still working at it. But even in the first year, my husband and children noticed remarkable changes. So did I.

Three practices that I've found I need to do to overcome negativity are:

1. Break the "baditude" habit. Start by taking the Complaint-Free Challenge.[10] Use a bracelet you already own or a rubber band. The whole point is to prayerfully become aware of your complaining, criticizing, and gossiping habits and be open to the Holy Spirit's conviction.

2. Replace "baditude" with God's Word. I found that just stopping myself from complaining wasn't enough; I needed something to replace the negativity running through my mind. Rehearsing ANCHOR verses is a great way to interrupt the negative patterns.

3. Replace "baditude" with gratitude. If you don't currently have a gratitude practice, start one. Begin with a simple gratitude journal, listing one thing you're grateful for each day. If you're already in this habit, start increasing the number of items you write down. Make it a competition with yourself to double, triple, even increase by tenfold!

One Rebel's Story, Part 2

The irritations will come. I can't change that.

But what if my perspective changed? What if I forgave them every single day, and let the irritations go—instead of swallowing hard and letting them build?

With my big kids, we've left the adorable, can't-do-wrong, let-me-hold-you-longer stage of motherhood. I miss it.

Now motherhood becomes a marathon of forgiveness. Or it should.

How might that morning (or others like it) change if I choose to forgive each frustration as it happens? Could I learn to see time spent talking through difficulties as a gift instead? A chance to lay foundations and build something beautiful in their hearts?

Oh, if only I could remember all the wrong I've done— the wrong I still do, and the way I'm fully forgiven.

Maybe then their childhood wouldn't need to be such a marathon of forgiveness.

Angie Parlin

Surfing the Emotion Ocean

We're at a bad news/good news moment. Here's the bad news: None of these suggestions actually worked for me the first time I tried them. Or even the tenth. Some took weeks just to put into practice. Then I spent months practicing and failing before I saw results.

But here's the good news: One day, a conflict occurred that normally would have caused me to flood with emotion. An hour later I realized, *Wait, what happened? More importantly, what didn't happen? Am I really on the other side of that incident, and I haven't lost my mind?*

Then I did what only those who share my struggles will understand: I wept with joy.

It works. It really works! I can change. I don't have to drown in the emotion ocean. I don't have to lose my mind!

This can happen for you too. Each time you stop trying harder on your own and take the little girl inside your heart to Jesus, the bullies have to back away. The more you practice facing those big emotion waves, the further away the bullies will stay.

Think back to your most recent episode of losing it. Replay it in your mind, only this time see yourself staying calm. Instead of being nearly drowned by big emotions, picture yourself hopping on a surfboard and surfing that wave for all it's worth.

As you start living braver, you will become a woman who loses her mind in the best possible way. Whose thoughts and feelings are totally transformed from fear to love. This really can happen for you.

One surrender at a time.

Tiny Acts of Rebellion

1. I will count to ten when I feel myself getting upset. One hundred if necessary. Or a thousand.

2. I will treat the little girl in my heart with tenderness, taking her to Jesus as many times as she needs.

3. I will add three or more things to my gratitude list every day.

4. I will share my concerns with God in prayer rather than venting to those around me.

5. I will give myself the time and space I need to navigate big emotions.

Tips for Each Rebel Type

Expressive

You tend to thrive on emotions and even enjoy embellishing them. Beware of your tendency to play drama queen. Many people find such performances draining. When someone shares with you how they're feeling, you may tend to respond, "You know, that reminds me of when I felt that way and…" But remember that they came to you to be heard, not to hear a story about you. Learn to let go of grudges. Otherwise, new experiences will continually trigger the old emotions, tempting you to overreact to everything rather than responding to the immediate event.

Analytic

You tend to be very private about your feelings and inner life. You can also feel very hurt by others' insensitivity to your feelings, unaware that others have no clue what you are feeling because you are not expressing them in a way they can read. While you don't have to become emotional, you do need to learn to speak clearly about your feelings rather than hinting and hoping that's enough. Don't automatically discount those who express big emotions more dramatically than you; it's not necessarily a sign of weakness, just a different way of communicating than you'd personally choose.

Driver

You equate vulnerability with weakness. So you generally try to avoid or ignore emotions, whether your own or others'. If the Performancism bully is in charge of your life, he'll make sure you stay crazy-busy so you never feel your own emotions or notice anyone else's. Don't wait until an illness or injury debilitates you, forcing you to stop and face what's inside. And don't wait until broken relationships force you to realize that other people's emotions aren't just a waste of your valuable time. Learn to accept and metabolize emotions.

Amiable

One of your assets is a deep sense of empathy. Because of this, you tend to not only easily identify but also absorb others' feelings. When someone you care about is experiencing and expressing big emotions, you can become overwhelmed to the point of paralysis. Remember, you don't have to own another's feelings in order to support them. Also, you tend to believe that in order to have the peace you crave, no negative feelings can be present. This is an unrealistic absolute. Learn to live in the tension of opposites—joy and sorrow, gratitude and disappointment—so circumstances can't control your peace.

Fun Is Not a Four-Letter Word

Giving yourself permission to have fun and still get things done.

✳

"We must risk delight.
We can do without pleasure, but not delight.
Not enjoyment.
We must have the stubbornness to accept our gladness
in the ruthless furnace of this world."

Poet Jack Gilbert

> **Bully belief 5:** "No fun until my work is done."

Daniel and the kids are watching a comedy DVD upstairs.

Without me (Cheri).

Oh, they invited me to join them.

As if I have time to spare.

"Take a break, Mom. Come have some fun with us!"

Easy for them to say.

As each fresh wave of laughter pours down the stairs, I ratchet my fuming up another notch.

I'm the one who's supposed to be an Expressive: fun is more important to me, and yet I'm sacrificing it. Where do they get off flaunting so much fun within my earshot? How can they just waste time like this when there's clearly so much that needs to get done? Nobody understands how hard I work to keep it all together around here. I can't afford to take a break. If I did, I'd just fall farther behind than I already am!

When the video is over, they all traipse down to the kitchen, still giggling, quoting lines, and sharing jokes known only by "fun club" members. Of which I am clearly not one.

141

Some nights, I fight back tears; others, I pick an argument. Every night, I wish for the freedom to walk away from all my "have tos" and enjoy a "want to."

It's a sad, paradoxical irony: for years, I've signed my emails "In His de-LIGHT" but lived like I'm carrying the weight of the world.

This was a regular scene in my life until I finally asked myself, "What is all this hard work and sacrifice getting me?" And the answer, to my dismay, was *nothing*. No worthwhile results. No lasting benefits. No accolades. No awards. Not even an occasional discount coupon.

And no happy memories to look back on. The fun times I allowed myself were few and far between. When looking at photos from family events, I couldn't even remember being there let alone any details about what happened. What had we talked about? Laughed about? Although physically present in the photos, I hadn't been able to relax, connect, and enjoy spending time with family.

What I could remember was everything I'd been stressing over and planning for during each event, as I'd counted the minutes until we could head home. So I could go back to getting important things done.

Your Relationship with Fun

For the following questions, circle all answers that apply to you. If something else comes to mind as you're thinking, write it in the "Other" blank.

Note: If fun is not something you inherently value, try substituting one of these words when responding: *delight, recreation, play, creativity,* or *celebration*.

1. When I was a child,
    a) my family had a lot of fun together.
    b) I found ways to have fun in spite of my family.
    c) fun was frowned upon as frivolous.
    d) I got in trouble for having too much fun.
    e) I was too busy to have much fun.
    f) I envied girls who had fun parents.
    g) Other:_____

2. Having fun doesn't seem
   a) necessary
   b) biblical
   c) Christian
   d) mature
   e) significant
   f) worthwhile
   g) Other:_____

3. I had more fun before
   a) I got married.
   b) I had children.
   c) I started working so many hours.
   d) an illness or injury.
   e) a crisis or emergency in my (our) life.
   d) a major loss in my (our) life.
   e) I went back to school.
   f) my latest move.
   g) Other:_____

4. I would have more fun now if only
   a) I had more time.
   b) I had more money.
   c) I had someone willing to have fun with me.
   d) I had more energy.
   e) I didn't have so much to do.
   f) I knew how.
   g) Other:_____

5. The main thing I do for fun these days is
   a) eat
   b) shop
   c) use social media
   d) watch TV shows or movies

    e) exercise

    f) take a nap

    g) Other:_____

6. If I don't start adding more fun into my life, I'm afraid that

    a) I'll become depressed.

    b) I'll be a cranky wife/mother/friend.

    c) I'll start looking for fun in all the wrong places.

    d) I'll miss out on my children's lives.

    e) my marriage will suffer.

    f) I'll look back with regret later.

    g) Other:_____

7. 10 Things I like doing just for fun:

    a) _____

    b) _____

    c) _____

    d) _____

    e) _____

    f) _____

    g) _____

    h) _____

    i) _____

    j) _____

This self-assessment has no score. It's just meant to help you reflect on your relationship to fun. But if you had any trouble filling in all ten for number 7, or if you skipped number 7 altogether, this chapter is for you.

What's the Big Deal About Fun?

For such a tiny word, *fun* has a huge range of meanings. Fun, like humor, is unique to each individual. Each of us finds different things funny. And each of us defines *fun* differently based on our family upbringing, personality, and season of life.

So let's start by getting clear on what we do and don't mean by *fun* in this chapter.

In his landmark book *First Things First*, Stephen Covey divided up all activities into four time quadrants: (1) Important and Urgent, (2) Important but Not Urgent, (3) Not Important but Urgent, and (4) Not Urgent and Not Important.[11] What we mean by *fun* in this chapter are activities that fall in Quadrant 2: Important but Not Urgent. Activities that involve recreation, creativity, play, celebration, or delight. We are not talking about activities that fall in Quadrant 4: Not Important and Not Urgent (indulgence, escape, time wasting).

Why Is All the Fun Gone?

The 2003 version of *Freaky Friday* with Jamie Lee Curtis and Lindsay Lohan has a memorable scene between Anna (the daughter) and Tess (the mother) that you may be repeating from memory already:

Anna (in Tess's body): "It's easy to be you. I'll just suck the fun out of everything."

Tess (in Anna's body): "I do not suck the fun out of everything."

Anna (in Tess's body): "Fun-sucker."[12]

None of us grew up wanting to become a fun-sucker. You've never waked up thinking, *How can I suck the fun out of everything today?* In fact, if you're like me, you get both teary and defensive at this scene, wanting to retort, "That's so unfair! I was fun once!"

If you ever find yourself wondering, "When did the fun stop?" or "Where did the fun go?" please know: these are vital questions.

Fun is often the first thing we let go when we're under pressure. If it's financial pressure, we cut fun out of the budget because we can't afford it. Time pressure? We don't have time.

Why else may fun be the first to go? See which of these more subtle reasons are true for you:

1. Self-punishment. We feel like we're not good enough to deserve rewards, so we deny ourselves actual fun. Then we feel so deprived, we indulge in escapes and time-wasters that don't actually provide any of the benefits of fun.

2. Martyrdom. We are the only one who understands that this project has to get done. Although we feel like we're sacrificing so much, it's merely pseudo-sacrifice because nobody needs it and nobody benefits. When our efforts go unappreciated, we become angry and bitter (see chapter 2).

3. Distrust of God. We say we trust God, but we're not sure if he'll come through, so we hedge our bets and try to do it all…just in case. Our desire to do it all is actually a form of self-protection.

4. Minimizing. We tell ourselves that fun can wait; we will always have more chances to have fun. But we end up creating a self-reinforcing system of denial. Since we so rarely have fun, we have no idea how many unique "you had to be there!" occasions we're missing.

5. Avoidance. We bury ourselves in work to avoid dealing with difficult relationships, perhaps at home or in our extended family. Obviously, avoiding others is socially unacceptable, but if you isolate because of work demands, you'll be lauded as responsible.

Why We Need Fun

Many of us consider fun to be frivolous, like the decorative frosting around a cake. It's a sweet treat at the edges of our lives, but certainly not central.

We're wrong.

Without fun, we can become ungrateful, critical, cynical, and even physically unhealthy. Conversely, fun enhances our lives in ways nothing else can. We feel better; laughter produces dopamine, a natural high. We develop community, fulfilling our needs for belonging and safety. We become more aware of God's continual goodness in our lives. And our physical health improves.

Is Fun a Godly Word?

Fun is not a major topic in the Bible. But we can find guiding principles related to fun throughout Scripture. Jesus's first miracle, for example, has long perplexed me. Of all things, why water to wine? Of all places, why a wedding? It seems so extravagant, frivolous, a waste of such an important "first."

But perhaps it's my interpretation that has been too shallow. Perhaps Jesus wanted to make it clear how important it is to stop working sometimes and celebrate.

Many Bible verses describe the benefits of joy, gladness, a cheerful heart, and delight as natural results of our relationship with God.

- "He will yet fill your mouth with *laughter* and your lips with shouts of *joy*" (Job 8:21).
- "The *joy* of the LORD is your strength" (Nehemiah 8:10).
- "The LORD is my strength and my shield; my heart *trusts* in him, and he helps me. My heart leaps for *joy*, and with my song I praise him" (Psalm 28:7).
- "But may the righteous *be glad* and *rejoice* before God; may they be *happy* and *joyful*" (Psalm 68:3).
- "A *cheerful* heart is good medicine" (Proverbs 17:22).
- "The *cheerful* heart has a continual feast" (Proverbs 15:15).
- "Trust in the LORD and do good; dwell in the land and enjoy safe pasture. Take *delight* in the LORD, and he will give you the desires of your heart" (Psalm 37:3-4).
- "Then I will go to the altar of God, to God, my *joy* and my *delight*. I will praise you with the lyre, O God, my God" (Psalm 43:4).

The verse that has challenged me the most in the last year is Matthew 5:16, "Let your light so shine before others, that they may see your good deeds and glorify your Father in heaven."

For most of my adult life, I fulfilled two-thirds of this verse. Oh, I let my light shine before others, all right. And you better believe I made certain that they saw my good works. But I experienced so little delight or joy in my work, I entirely missed the last part. The most important part. The part without which the first two-thirds not only doesn't matter but actually became destructively self-centered.

I've been late in discovering a crucial truth: a joyless Christian is a contradiction in terms.

Everyone Needs Some Fun

Repeat after me: Fun is not a luxury. It's a legitimate need.

Great start. Now, try these three ways to let fun out of exile and back into your life.

1. Add Fun to Your Schedule

A healthy, balanced diet involves a variety of different foods and flavors. In the same way, a healthy, balanced life includes a variety of activities, one of which is fun.

You take most seriously things that make it on your to-do list. If you're running low on fun, it's time to put it on your calendar.

One way to keep an eye on how you're doing with balance is to color code your to-do list or calendar so you can see at a glance where you've sprinkled it with fun and where there's an alarming deficit. Balance will look different for each one of us. It'll change based on your life seasons and situations. Adding fun to your schedule makes it more likely to happen.

2. Figure Out What's Fun for You

Many women we surveyed said the same thing about adding more fun to their lives: "I'd love to have more fun, but even if I made the time, I'm not sure what I'd do! How pathetic is that?"

Actually, it's not pathetic at all. It makes total sense. You've matured beyond much of what you found fun as a child or teen. But you've not discovered what you enjoy now. In order to have more fun, find out what's fun for you. The list you made on page 144 is a good place to start. Talk to friends to get ideas, especially those whose personalities are similar to yours.

Take a risk and try something new—something that involves recreation, play, creativity, celebration, or delight. We know it's a risk: if you don't know for sure that you'll enjoy it, why waste precious time only to end up disappointed? But the only way to know for sure is to give it a try.

That's how I found out that belly dancing only looked fun. My friend Shawna and I laughed until we cried while attempting the one class together, so it was totally worth it. But she went on to become a competitive Irish dancer, so taking this one risk led to a real passion for her.

I forced myself to take several card-making classes. But I finally realized that *trying so hard* to have fun really isn't fun. (The fact that the card aisle of Target made me want to weep tears of relief and shout, "I don't have to make them anymore!" was also a major clue.)

Reading comedian Andrea Coli's book about what improvisation taught her about God made me want to try improv. But I was way too chicken. (I like my spontaneity carefully planned, thank you.) In researching local improv classes, I found an instructor who taught both improv and solo performing classes. When I went to see a performance, I was mesmerized by the eight monologues, each written during a seven-week class. I didn't just find myself thinking, *I could do that. I had* to do it. I couldn't wait! Sure enough, solo performing has been a great fit for me, providing some of the most fun I've had in the last two years.

Leaving the house to take a class is great, but in certain seasons of life it isn't possible. You need plenty of fun things to do that fit in a five- to twenty-minute break. Here's a starter "Fun Break Idea List" we've compiled:

1. Watch a comedy clip on YouTube (we highly recommend Jeanne Robertson).
2. Fire up the Keurig and turn on HGTV.
3. Read a chapter (or two) in a novel.
4. Create a digital scrapbook page.
5. Read a blog post (or two).
6. Write a blog post.
7. Listen to a favorite song.
8. Take a bubble bath.
9. Call a friend to chat.
10. Change your nail polish color.
11. Update your Tumblr page.
12. Crank up the praise music; sing and dance for an audience of One.
13. Lie on the couch for a few minutes of quiet.
14. Take a walk or go for a run.

15. Savor a delicious treat.

16. Make progress on a craft project.

17. Make music.

18. Play a video game.

19. Try a new recipe.

20. Other: _____ (Keep adding!)

3. Play the Gratitude Game

Sometimes, we make changes in our lives so we can add new activities. Other times, we add new activities because they'll change our lives. Playing the Gratitude Game is a new activity that requires little time or energy but is guaranteed to make big changes.

The goal of the Gratitude Game is to celebrate God's abundant goodness (Psalm 145:7). The way you play is simple: just keep track of things you're grateful for throughout the day. I use a simple journal with an ever-growing list. Kathi's family writes each individual item on a slip of paper and adds it to a jar.

The only competition is with yourself. Start by noticing at least one thing you're grateful for each day. Then double it. At some point, increase to five a day. When that gets easy, go for ten. I've kept buying bigger and bigger journals and challenging myself to fill an entire page each day.

The best thing about the Gratitude Game is that everybody wins. You win because your awareness of God's blessings in your life increases. Your family wins because they hear you focusing on positives and sense you becoming more content.

And it's fun! Psalm 92:4 says,

> You make me glad by your deeds, LORD,
> I sing for joy at what your hands have done.

And Psalm 126:2 says,

> Our mouths were filled with laughter,
> our tongues with songs of joy.

Then it was said among the nations,
"The LORD has done great things for them."

One Rebel's Story

No fun till your work is done. But the work never ends! There is always another load of laundry, a dishwasher to unload, a meal to make, a kid to pick up, an errand to run, a bed to make, a cat to feed, and dog to walk. When is it time for me? The moment I walk down the hall for bed? I tap out words with friends on my phone. Sigh. This is not enough for my creative soul.

It is a work of love to run my home. I enjoy the creative ways I feed my family or show them love with clean clothes. But seriously, I need something more. Something fun.

Knitting is my guilty pleasure. And I do feel guilt every time I pick up my needles when there are dirty dishes in the sink. Yet a happy woman is better at serving her family, so I have developed some blindness. I turn my back to the dishes. I let plants go unwatered. I make dinner in the slow cooker. I knit between loads of laundry.

I need those rows to calm my soul. I can do just about anything after a few rows of wool between my fingers. It takes discipline to let the chore wait and silence the voice in my head telling me I'm a bad person. But I am so much better with a smile on my face coming from a little creative time than I am as a cranky person wondering when it will be my time to play. Hard as it is to take twenty minutes for me first, I do it. And you know what? My chores sometimes go faster and I can sneak in another few rows while I'm making dinner and waiting in the carpool line.

Treat yourself to a little me time, just twenty minutes. Honestly, the chores are relentless and will always be there. Putting a smile on your face is the better option.

Lisa Bogart

Fun Is Worth Fighting For

We wrote this book during crazy-busy seasons of both our lives. I was teaching, taking a qualitative research course, preparing talks for several upcoming retreats, hosting girls' Bible study groups in my home, and getting ready for a trip to England. Kathi was writing a different book, preparing for Mom Con, speaking at Hearts at Home, starting a podcast, and preparing for and recovering from major surgery.

If we'd listened to the bullies, we would have postponed all fun until January 21, 2014, the day after our deadline. Instead, in late August 2013, we chose to drop everything and attend a Shakespeare play together. We almost cancelled at the last minute, as we'd both been sick and felt terribly behind on all we had to do.

I'll admit, the "no fun until the work is done" belief felt so sensible at the time. After all, it would free up much needed time. I even texted Kathi, "We can always rain check 'til next season." But we decided to go. We had a wonderful time seeing *Taming of the Shrew* and talking about marriage (of all things).

A week later, Shakespeare Santa Cruz announced they were closing their doors for good. If we'd postponed because of all the work we still had left to do, we would have had no next season.

Was it easy? No.

Was it worth it? Totally.

Did I get all my work done? Not even. I rescheduled several things and deleted others.

Do I remember any of them right now? Haven't got a clue. But I remember laughing my head off with Daniel, Kathi, and Roger that Saturday night in August.

Be intentional about having fun. Remember that love and laughter go hand in hand. Don't let fear turn you into an unconscious fun-sucker. Stop trying harder to get your work done so you can finally have fun. Start living braver: fight for fun now.

It's worth it.

You're worth it. You're already a daughter of God's delight. Become a rebel who is known for her cheerful heart. For her contagious laughter. And especially for her joy.

Tiny Acts of Rebellion

1. I will offer a big smile to the next person I see.
2. I will start a fun jar for myself. Today I'll add one idea, and I'll keep adding until I have a collection of 101 ways that I enjoy having fun.
3. I will ask a friend about her favorite ways of having fun.
4. I will share a funny ecard or video online.
5. I will call up a relative and say, "Remember when…?" until we're both laughing.

Tips for Each Rebel Type

Expressive

You must have fun, and one of your assets is your ability to create fun where there is none. You can turn almost any task into a game, improving group morale. Since your need for fun is greater than any other personality, you will need to take responsibility for making sure this need is met. Don't waste time or energy waiting for others to plan some fun or resenting those who don't join in. Focus on those who want to have fun with you and get that party started!

Analytic

When the Perfectionism bully is breathing down your neck, it can keep you working around the clock. After all, there simply is not enough time in an ordinary day to do absolutely everything you need to do to the high standard of "perfect." Throw in an emergency or two, and fun will get crowded out of your life for weeks, months, even years. The physical, mental, spiritual, and emotional benefits of fun are more than worth the time required. It may seem like wasted time in the moment, but it's actually one of the best ways to invest your time.

Driver

For you, work is fun. You thrive on having lots to do and moving at a high pace. As long as the Performancism bully isn't calling the shots, you can enjoy your fun while you're getting your work done. Keep in mind that not everyone is like this; others will need time off from work in order to have fun. And beware of burnout. When you have to force yourself to work, it's time to step back from work and focus on fun. If you don't, you may find yourself incapable of working or having fun because your body and mind are so worn down.

Amiable

You're always glad to join in the fun, as long as you're not expected to take charge. Your idea of fun tends to be more low-key than for other personalities. You consider just hanging out together plenty of fun; it doesn't cost much or require much preparation. You prefer spontaneous fun, such as a spur-of-the-moment road trip, to carefully orchestrated fun. You'd rather see what happens than have a schedule of exactly what is supposed to happen. A large part of fun for you is the serendipity of unplanned surprises. Other personalities will need more structure; find ways to cooperate with them without conforming to their detailed plans.

CHAPTER 14

Give Yourself a Time Out

Everyone (and we mean *everyone*) needs a nap.

※

"Each person deserves a day away in which no problems are confronted, no solutions searched for. Each of us needs to withdraw from the cares which will not withdraw from us."

MAYA ANGELOU, *Wouldn't Take Nothing for My Journey Now*

> **Bully belief 6:** "I'll rest when I'm dead."

"This stupid computer!"

Ugh. I (Kathi) love my computer—my "time-saving device"—but for a while there it was as slow as molasses.

In winter.

In Minnesota.

But I have a secret weapon whenever my computer is wonky. My husband's a software architect. (Yeah, I've tried to understand his title as well. All I know is that he works in software, works with a lot of teams to get the results he needs, and is really smart.) So whenever I have a tech glitch on my laptop, all I need to do is hand it to Roger and say, "Make it go." And he does.

But after this happened several times, he finally said, "You know that what I do 99 percent of the time is just shut down all your programs and restart your computer. You could do the same thing."

Which really bothered me. You see, I don't have time for my computer to not be functioning at full capacity. I need my computer to do what I need it to do when I need it. I don't have time to close windows I'm not using and reboot when the computer is not performing to capacity.

And this faulty thinking about my computer is just like the faulty thinking I've had about myself. *It doesn't matter how many windows I have open. It doesn't matter how many tasks I have going at the same time.* Like my computer:

1. I am better doing one thing at a time.

2. I need to shut down regularly in order to fully function when I am on.

Take the Rest Test

Fill in each blank with the first thing that comes to mind:

1. I get _____ hours of sleep each night.

2. I drink no more than _____ caffeinated beverages a day to keep me alert.

3. When I'm feeling sleepy or exhausted, I _____ drive.

4. I make sure to exercise _____ minutes each day.

5. I _____ take brain breaks of five to ten minutes just to clear my head.

6. If I feel sleepy in the afternoon, I _____.

7. I work _____ hours a day.

8. I have _____ hours of discretionary time each day.

9. Once a week, I take _____ hours off for rest.

10. I _____ take truly restful vacations (or staycations.)

Reflecting on your answers:

1. Most women need eight or more hours of sleep per night.

2. Using any artificial methods to stay awake is a warning sign.

3. The safest answers are "don't" or "ask someone else to."

4. Even fifteen to twenty minutes of mild aerobic exercise can help you sleep far better at night.

5. "Never" is a red-flag answer.

6. "Take a quick nap," "take a quick walk," and "drink a glass of water" are all healthy answers.

7. More than eight to ten hours takes a toll on all aspects of your life.

8. While there's no one right answer here, you need margins in your life—spaces for the unexpected and the necessary to take priority without causing even more stress.

9. Twenty-four is an excellent spiritual discipline.

10. "Regularly" is the answer we're looking for. ("Never" is not!)

One Thing at a Time

Multitasking is the great lie of the twenty-first century. While research has shown that men tend to think about one thing at a time (and no, *that* is not all he thinks about), women usually are thinking about several things at once. But that doesn't mean we are good at *doing* several things at once.

Part of the reason we feel on edge (I like to describe it as "my hair is hurting") is that we've set up unreasonable expectations about the amount of work we should be able to get done, without taking other factors into consideration:

- "I should be able to get this report written while my two-year-old naps in the other room."

- "I should be able to cook dinner in the fifteen minutes we are home between school and rugby practice."

- "I should be able to clean out my daughter's room and then paint it today."

Any time your thought or conversation starts with "I should be able to…" check to see if you're setting up an unreasonable expectation for yourself. When we expect to get too much done in a day, we start cutting out the luxuries (a nap, time with our husband, playing with the dog, exercise, reading) to catch up on the things we "should have been able to get done."

There is no rest in trying to do everything at once. No beginning and no end.

Shutting Down So We Can Be Fully On

Not only do we need to stop trying to do too many things at once, but we need to also genuinely rest when we have the opportunity. When we don't rest, the very thing we're killing ourselves over starts to suffer. That project for work that you're staying up until midnight to complete—it just gets more difficult to work on the less rest you have.

How do you know if you're not getting enough rest? Here are some clues that tell me I'm experiencing diminishing returns on my overexertion:

- It takes me twice as long to finish a project as it would when I'm rested.
- I end up rereading a paragraph multiple times to get the meaning of it.
- I don't schedule late afternoon meetings because I know I won't be fully present.
- I repeat phrases to myself like, "Don't be such a wimp," and "Suck it up, Buttercup," just so I'll push through on a project.
- I keep extending my work hours because I need to get so much more done.

One Rebel's Story

Author Stephanie Shott knows the hamster wheel, "I'll rest when I'm dead."

"No worries. I'll rest when I'm dead."

That has been my default response to every concerned friend who tells me I really need to slow down and get some rest. That's because the whole *rest* thing is much easier said than done when there's always so much to do. So, my days begin before the crack of dawn and end somewhere around

1:00 a.m. I know it's pretty hard to be an early bird and a night owl in the same skin, but what's a girl to do when her plate overfloweth and her to-do list never ends.

Unfortunately that's not just true for me, it's true for the majority of women on the planet. We busy ourselves with the business of each day, and then we find ourselves over-booked, overworked, and overwhelmed.

But it doesn't take long to figure out that we weren't cre-ated for perpetual production and an incessant work sched-ule. The consequences of living life in fifth gear without taking an occasional break has a way of taking its toll.

Desperate to meet deadlines, frantic to fulfill every need, and adamant about making every appointment, we are drowning in the sea of our own busyness and yet, we won't stop long enough to come up for air.

For me, it's often all in the name of ministry that I try to do it all and end up feeling frazzled, scattered, weary, worn out, and overwhelmed. Wanting to accomplish it all yet not accomplishing much well. Longing to be thorough but too busy to pay attention to details.

Wondering what happened to long lunches with friends, walks on the beach with my man, and movie days in bed, yet never stopping long enough to enjoy them.

God created us to need physical, mental, and emotional rest for a reason. So, "I'll rest when I'm dead" isn't really a good answer.

Through my crazy-busy years of doing too much for my britches, I discovered that when we don't get enough rest, it affects us, body, soul, and spirit. It affects our relationships, our productiveness, and our perspective. What starts as ser-vice to God can damage and even replace our relationship with God.

And if we don't get enough rest, our lack of rest may just force us to a place where we won't have a choice.

It's so true. Saying no is the first step to rest. The second step is to actually plan your rest.

Rest Is a Gift—and a Command

Daily Rest

I just woke up from a nap, and it feels glorious.

I used to think naps were for wimps. Then I started to read the work of Tony Schwartz, author of *Be Excellent at Anything* and founder of www.theenergyproject.com, and realized that powerful people all over the world are bringing their pillows and blankies to their corner offices to grab a few minutes of shut-eye.[13] Companies are reporting that when their employees take an afternoon siesta, they are significantly happier and more productive than those without naps.

But how does this translate to your real life?

Scheduling even fifteen minutes to put your head down on your desk, or fall asleep in your car (while it's parked, of course), or napping when your kids nap can make a significant improvement to your day. But be sure to set the alarm on your cellphone. You don't want to be waking up as everyone else is going home from work.

Weekly Rest

God has promised that six days of the week are sufficient to accomplish what he has given us to do. The final day is a gift for us to share with him.

> "Remember the Sabbath day by keeping it holy. Six days you shall labor and do all your work, but the seventh day is a sabbath to the LORD your God. On it you shall not do any work…For in six days the LORD made the heavens and the earth, the sea, and all that is in them, but he rested on the seventh day. Therefore the LORD blessed the Sabbath day and made it holy" (Exodus 20:8-11).

God knows exactly how he designed us—to work hard and then to rest well. But he also knows that overworking is driven by fear. ("What if I don't get everything done?" "What if I haven't done everything I need to do for my family?") He knows that when someone says "You need to rest," our tendency is to reply, "Don't worry, I'm fine."

But God knows better what we need than we do ourselves. "Sabbath is a gift—but we are so reluctant to accept it that God had to make it a command," says Barbara Brown Taylor.

Once a week, we need to pull back. Seven days a week is not only not healthy, it's not trusting God for the amount he has given us to do.

Developing New Restful Habits

Yesterday was my last speaking event for the year. Today's date? November 10.

Normally I will pack in events until the week before Christmas. I love what I do, speaking and traveling, but I've finally come to the conclusion that I'm a much better speaker when I speak less, not more.

As I was growing my speaking ministry, I would take any opportunity that came along. If you wanted me to pay my own way to get to your church, I would do it. Want me to sleep on the couch in your living room with your three cats? Bring it on.

Until I realized I didn't like speaking anymore.

Well, that wasn't true. The truth is, I was exhausted. I was living by the credo that there is always time to rest, replenish, and renew "later on," as in,

- "I'll stay up all night preparing this presentation for work, and I can catch up on sleep later on."

- "I'll say yes to the request for volunteers at my kid's school because I do have two hours open on Saturday."

- "When my kids ask me to drive them and their friends to the mall, I say yes without hesitation because I want to be a good mom, and that's what good moms do."

But I've come to realize that in saying yes to so many people, instead of feeling like I've "paid those people off" and I don't owe a favor anymore, I'm laying down a path for them to come to me with any whim, need, or desire. I may not be the right person to meet their need, but I've told the world that the path of least resistance leads to me.

It was a big church and a big deal. Big Church wanted me to come speak to their moms' group. Actually, four of their moms' groups.

"We can't pay you, and you'll have to get your own hotel room, but we see you're going to be speaking at another church in our area the night before, so it wouldn't be that much extra cost. We know that our moms would love you, and it would be a huge ministry to them if you came to speak."

Translation: We won't pay you, but you should do it anyway.

My first instinct is to always try to make something work. Is there a way I could work it out so that I could speak to their groups? I love to minister to moms and always want to help a group in need.

But Roger and I had set some boundaries earlier in the year: I needed to build more rest into my schedule, so I needed to speak to a limited number of groups and only to those that were able to pay the agreed-upon fee unless it was a special circumstance, I had to send a note back saying I would not be able to speak to their group.

That did not sit well with Big Church.

The same day I sent the email saying I needed to decline, one of Big Church's members happened to be at the same conference I was speaking at. I was chatting with a group of women, and this leader from Big Church barreled into the middle of the conversation and said, "Why won't you speak for our group, even though you're going to be in town anyway? Is it all about the money for you?"

Everyone in the little group stood there in stunned silence. After breathing deeply, I said to her, "Wow, I don't think this is the right time to talk about this. How about you come back at the close of the conference and we can talk then?"

She walked away in a righteous huff.

And, because I want people to like me, I felt overwhelming guilt that I had to disappoint this group. It wasn't until I told my husband what had happened that my guilt turned to anger.

"Would they be okay if they were asked to work for free?" Roger said. "How about if their husbands were asked to come into work for no pay on the weekends, when they would want to spend time together as a family? And then trying to make you feel guilty for saying no? Just because you're in the same town doesn't mean that all your time is up for grabs. You need time to rest just like anyone else. Unbelievable!"

It was a perspective I'd never really considered before. No one had the right to demand my time. I always just figured, everyone is busy, so I should be too.

Even if it meant I spent less time with my family.

Even if it meant I was tired and strung out.

Even if it meant I was cutting corners on things that are important to me, like spending time with friends and family or just hanging out with my dog.

I'd fallen for the trap that so many of us fall into: If I have a blank spot on my calendar and someone wants it, I should be willing to give it to them. It never occurred to me that maybe that blank spot needed to be dedicated to rest.

God puts a high priority on rest, and if I don't protect my rest, no one else will. There is never a reason to feel guilty for taking care of your health.

What does rest look like?

The inbox is just sitting there, taunting me. It's Sunday, and I know there are people waiting for answers from me. I was gone all day Friday and Saturday, and the emails piled up while I was away. I'm under attack from all the shoulds.

I should answer those emails.

I should run errands today so Monday isn't so crazy.

I should return phone calls now.

And I'm just worn out.

To take a day off, a day that God has set aside for rest, feels radical and subversive. To take a day of Sabbath feels about as countercultural as saying, "I don't own a computer, I use a manual typewriter for all my correspondence."

And it's a double-edged sword, this rest thing. People in my life have recognized the need for years. "You work too hard." "You're always going, going, going!" But as soon as I try to put some boundaries in my life, those very same people are frustrated with me. "You never have time for me anymore."

Everyone wants you to rest. Just not when they need you.

It takes courage to rest when the world tells you they are going to just die without you. Rarely do I see it just happen—that all my worlds line up and there's suddenly a day with nothing on my schedule, nothing on my to-do list, no one needing me.

But if I don't sometimes leave things half done, I will never get the rest I need and that God commands.

Rebels Make Rest a Reality

Rebels Plan a Day of Rest

God commanded rest. If week after week goes by and you are never able to have a day to rest, something is wrong with your schedule. When I work on the weekends, I'll choose a weekday to be my Sabbath. I will not schedule meetings, work, or phone calls on that day. I will read, cook, see a friend, have dinner with my husband, do a more in-depth Bible reading, listen to the sermon from my church online, and generally plan to slow down my day. On my day of rest, I do things that shake me out of my day-to-day routine and restore my spirit.

But as often as I can, I make Sunday my day of rest. On those days I try to have lunch or dinner prepped in advance (or we keep it really simple, just soup or sandwiches for lunch). Once we get home from church and eat, there is often napping involved, followed by having our extended family over for a simple meal.

Stop Confusing "Rest Day" with "Catch-Up Day"

Does that feel unrealistic? Yep. Do I sometimes throw in a load of underwear on Sunday? Yes.

But from sundown on Saturday to sundown on Sunday, I don't plan on *accomplishing* anything. I'm retraining my brain to not factor those hours into checking things off and getting things done. Sometimes I cook and bake, not because that's the plan, but that's how I connect with my family. Sometimes I run errands, but I do it with my husband because it sounds like a great way to spend time together.

Finding Real Rest

Today God slapped me upside the head and then gave me a kiss on the cheek, as only he can do.

The list of household stuff that I need to get done is just huge, and there is nothing I hate more than stripping sheets and remaking the bed, and the *whole* thing needed to be done. Down to the dust ruffle. So there I was, grumbling and complaining.

And then God kept giving me pictures of the ministry that happens in that place:

It's where God provides rest for me more nights than not.

It's where I fall asleep on the shoulder of the man he has given me to demonstrate his love in a tangible way.

It's where I've loved my kids, read his Word, and recovered when I was sick.

This is going to sound silly, but I am now taking time to "dress" the bed. Hanging the comforter to dry in the sun so it smells like only sun-dried cloth can. Fluffing the pillows, spraying the linens (I'm talking Home Good specials, nothing fancy, but comfy), folding the quilts, and making it as comfy as possible for me and my husband.

And I ended up grateful to God for providing so richly and valuing rest and connection so deeply. And I prayed that when you, dear reader, laid your head down tonight, you would feel restored and cherished by the love of God.

> The Lord is my shepherd, I lack nothing.
>> He makes me lie down in green pastures,
> he leads me beside quiet waters,
>> he refreshes my soul.
>> (Psalm 23:1-3)

Why is it that we spend money that we don't have to buy clothes for the rest of the world to see, but we replace our pillows only once a decade. Our rest priorities are messed up.

We try so hard to get everything done that we neglect our own needs and, in the process, even God's commands.

One way to start living braver is self-care through rest. I hope you'll take rest seriously. We can change the world—as long as we get our naps in beforehand.

Tiny Acts of Rebellion

1. I will take a nap—even if it's not Sunday.

2. I will listen to music instead of accomplishing something on my to-do list while I wait in my car for my kids.

3. I will take a day off this week to go to church, rest, and play with my family.

4. I will radically mark out time on my calendar for something I love: reading, hiking, or going to the movies.

Tips for Each Rebel Type

Expressive

As an extrovert, you gain energy from other people. And you certainly add lots of fun and enthusiasm to any group you're in. However, beware of your tendency to seek a "people high" when you feel yourself dragging. You do need time alone to rest and recuperate. And as much as you love talking, you also need to learn the value of silence, both for yourself (so you can actually listen for a while) and for others (so you don't talk their ear off).

Analytic

You probably know all the statistics about how many hours of sleep you need. But you intentionally ignore the facts because you still have so much to do. You've not achieved perfection. There are still so many wrongs yet to be righted in your part of the world. The problem with this approach is that you tend to exhaust yourself while doing acts of great love. But all that others remember is your exhaustion, not the love you were demonstrating. So make rest a priority for your own sake and theirs.

Driver

Since one of your major assets is energy, you may think that rest is for wimps and sleep is a total waste of time. One of your liabilities is your tendency to ignore that your body, mind, and spirit need to detach from work and recharge. New brain research even suggests that sleep releases toxins from your brain. Put "rest" and "sleep" on your schedule so that you take them seriously and can enjoy the adrenaline rush of checking them off your list.

Amiable

Of all the personalities, you most naturally enjoy rest. But you're often made to feel guilty, as if rest is lazy. Be aware that not all rest is created equal. There's a huge difference between resting for the purpose of re-creation and doing nothing as a means of escape. One restores while the other weakens. Limit the time you spend with Quadrant 4 time-wasters. Also, learn to advocate for your rest needs while on vacations or trips with those who have higher energy. You don't have to be dragged hither and yon to the point of exhaustion just because that's what others enjoy.

CHAPTER 15

Disappointment Isn't Deadly

Learning to say, "I'm sorry you're sad, but I'm not buying you a pony."

✳

*"No man is fit to command another that
cannot command himself."*

WILLIAM PENN

Bully belief 7: "I'm responsible for everyone else's happiness."

I (Kathi) want you to like me.

I really, really want you to like me. You may call it needy. I call it being human. I am okay, however, with some people not liking me.

- People who don't tip waitresses well.
- People who still shop at Abercrombie & Fitch.
- People who are mean on the Internet.
- Wine snobs.

But for the most part, if you have a pulse, I would rather that you like me. And that is why it's almost physically painful for me to say no to people. At some point, it becomes exhausting. This carrying the weight of the world on your shoulders.

And how did I recognize it in myself? It took my dog to point out how very codependent I am.

Jake is a puggle (a pug-beagle mix) that we rescued several years ago from our local dog shelter. At the adoption center, he looked like any bright, happy pup waiting for a forever home. We loved him immediately and filled out the forms after only two visits.

But as soon as we got home, we had an inkling why Jake may have been returned as damaged goods. Jake was a very nervous dog. He would not leave my or my husband's side while we were in the house. He got very anxious anytime anyone else was in the house, including our sons. If we left the house, he would go into the very corner of our bathroom, hide behind the toilet, and shake uncontrollably until we got home.

Jake had issues, but some of his issues also seemed very sweet. Jake can't stand to see me upset. If Roger and I are having a discussion about money (which can be a very stressful subject for me), or if I have a situation with one of my kids that's weighing me down, or even if I just decide to watch the opening scene of the movie *Up* (you know, where the man falls in love with his wife, and they show their love through the years, and then his wife dies...I could cry just typing about it), Jake feels as if it's his responsibility to fix it.

He will snuggle into my lap (all thirty-five pounds of him) and push his nose under my hand to get me to pet him. If that doesn't stop the crying, Jake will start nudging me to come play with him or bring me a rawhide as a little cheer up treat.

And the whole time, I can hear Jake's internal monologue: "Don't be sad, Mommy. Don't cry. Look, I'll snuggle with you! Look, I'll do tricks for you! Don't cry!"

So I just sit there and try to make Jake feel better. I pet him and try to put on a happy face and let him know that everything will be okay. So instead of crying out my cry, I'm now all worried about how Jake is doing.

You see, all Jake wants in life is to be surrounded by people he loves and for all of them to just be *chill*. His main priority in life is to have a peaceful home—even if everyone has to fake it.

Oh, I am so like my friend Jake. How about you?

Fill in the blanks below with *always, frequently, sometimes, rarely,* or *never*.

1. I _____ try to soften the blow when my child has a disappointment.
2. I _____ try to make sure my husband is in a good mood.
3. I _____ believe that others will know what I want and need if they really care.

4. I am _____ the one who keeps the peace in my circle of friends or coworkers.

5. When people aren't getting along, I _____ feel the need to mediate.

6. I _____ feel unappreciated for the sacrifices I make on behalf of others.

7. If there's a fine line between wanting to be a part of people's joy and happiness, and feeling responsible for their joy and happiness, I cross it _____.

8. I _____ feel like a bad mom when my kids don't get along.

9. I _____ think to myself, *If I had just said the right thing the right way, nobody would be upset.*

10. I _____ try to prevent those I love from experiencing pain, even the pain of natural consequences.

11. I _____ keep quiet about my own wants and needs.

12. I am _____ the peacekeeper with my adult family members.

13. I _____ feel resentful when others don't seem to realize how hard I'm trying to make everything work out for them.

14. I hate conflict and _____ try to avoid it.

15. I _____ word my input as a helpful question (such as, "Are you sure you want to do it that way?") rather than a statement.

And the dangerous aspect to all of this is that we live with the illusion that we have some measure of control over how other people behave. We're like a three-year-old kid strapped into his car seat and using his Fisher-Price steering wheel, absolutely certain that he's the one driving the car.

It's crazy feeling that we have all the responsibility for other people's lives, with none of the authority to make a difference. Such a frustrating way to go through life!

Try-Harder Living vs. Living Braver

In Try-Harder Living, we live under the illusion that if we can just say the right thing in the right way, everyone will get along, be happy, and like us. Sounds oversimplistic, but many of us run our lives with that illusion.

There are real reasons why we behave this way. Perhaps your parents weren't as functional as they needed to be and you were saddled with too much responsibility too young. That can show up later in life as trying to control situations because that was how you were trained. You don't know any other way to function in your family.

When I was in college, I worked at a tuxedo store. We sold and rented tuxes and all the accessories. Rick, one of the guys in my college group at church, called me at work and asked if I could hook him up with a low-cost tux to rent for our church event the next night. I told him that I would need to check with the owner, but I didn't think so. But because I wanted to be nice, I told him I would ask.

The owner ended up with a personal emergency that day and never came in to work. I called Rick to let him know it wasn't going to work because the owner wasn't coming in. "Great," Rick said. "He'll never know. I'll be by in an hour to get fitted." And then he hung up on me.

One of my coworkers, Scott, overheard the whole thing. I was freaking out because I would never steal from my company, but I was almost ready to throw up at the thought of having to confront Rick. I considered paying for the tux rental myself so that no one would be mad at me. That's when Scott told me to go to the break room and get some water.

When Rick came into the store, Scott let him have it with both barrels. "Kathi says you're a friend from church, but I find that hard to believe. Anyone who knows her would know that she would never give away merchandise for free that wasn't hers. You need to make other tux arrangements."

Scott was able to do what it's taken me decades to figure out: anyone who wants to take advantage of me isn't a friend worth sacrificing for. Or perhaps you (as most of us) were never taught great personal boundaries so it is easy to let others take advantage of you now.

One Rebel's Story

"I've never had a truly happy day in my life," my oldest son said at age ten. My heart dropped at those words.

Marcel Proust said, "Let us be grateful to the people who make us happy; they are the charming gardeners who make our souls blossom."

Beautiful sentiments—charming gardeners, souls blossoming—yet how wrong Proust is. It is a false job, this gardener making us happy. There is a difference between bringing sunshine into someone's day through kind acts and taking responsibility for maintaining another's happiness level. With Proust's assertion, if I am unhappy, it's because someone didn't work hard enough to make me happy. It's not my fault; it's yours.

Is happiness contingent on the efforts of others? Is my happiness your job? Is my child, spouse, or parent's happiness my job?

Until my boys turned ten, I could create a controlled bubble of happiness. Like a traffic controller, I could avert meltdowns, coach away from poor choices, balance a bad day with an extra dose of good.

At ten, though, independence starts showing itself in the garden of their life. Suddenly, they're holding the bulb of happiness in their hands—and don't quite know how to make it work.

Instead of teaching my son to soar, I became an enabler. By not teaching him how to grow his own happiness, I had clipped his wings.

Coax a child out of the doldrums, and you make him happy for a moment. Teach a child to find his own, and you've given him the tools to be happy for a lifetime.

There isn't enough of me to go around being the charming gardener making sure souls blossomed happiness.

Happiness is a Soul Flower that to possess, one must grow themselves.

Mary Leigh Bucher

And the most dangerous part of this? We teach our kids and those around us to take on responsibility for those around them to the neglect of themselves. This has been labeled Christian.

Recently, I was chatting with my daughter Kimberly. We were talking about her plans for college in the coming fall, including money issues, and she was obviously in a tender spot and feeling judged. I asked her a question about some plans she and her brother, Justen, had talked about for the weekend, and out of the blue she said, "I hate having to be the go-between for everyone else all the time."

Where did that come from? My husband and I had worked hard to make sure that the kids in our blended family didn't feel put in the middle of anything—whether it was with their other parents, their brothers and sisters, or the outside world.

Even though Kimber wasn't getting the message from us that she needed to be the go-between for the family, she had seen me live it out day to day, and assumed the responsibility.

If that doesn't make me want to change my ways, nothing will.

God Doesn't Promise a Pain-Free Life

Our wanting to make everything okay for everyone around us springs from the best of intentions: we hate to see others in pain. We would never intentionally hurt someone else. But God never promised us a problem-free life, and we should not expect it for ourselves or the people around us.

Problems are a part of life. That's how we grow. John 16:33 says, "I have told you these things, so that in me you may have peace. In this world you will have trouble. But take heart! I have overcome the world."

Recently, my son was having some trouble with some paperwork at his contract job. He was frustrated and moody about the situation, and I hated to see him that way. I know the person he was dealing with, so I was tempted to call and see if I could fix the issue.

But I resisted.

Oh, it was so hard. I wanted to make sure that Justen was okay—I hate to see my kid in pain. But I also had to realize that this was a growing opportunity for him. I literally had to sit on my hands to not email my friend to see if I could help.

And you know what? The situation is working out. Yes, it took a little extra effort, and it refocused me on my best role in Justen's life—his prayer warrior.

Pain Is a Growth Opportunity

I hate a growth opportunity—for me or anyone I love.

I have some really twisted thinking. I understand that the only way I've truly grown in life is to survive the hard stuff. But then I desperately want anyone I love not to have to experience any hurt, pain, or trauma.

When I was a teen, I read a story about a man who was stricken with polio as an elementary schooler. Sadly, the polio outbreak had hit much of their community and several of his classmates were also attacked by the disease, which could lead to paralysis, deformity, life in an iron lung, or even death.

Every night, this young man's mother would perform the heartbreaking task of stretching his muscles so they would not atrophy. These were not simple stretches. Each movement was incredibly painful for her young son. It took everything within her to not cry while performing these exercises because she knew the pain she was inflicting. She would wait until their session was done and quietly cry behind her closed bedroom door.

One day she was waiting at school to pick up her son and was chatting with another mom whose son was also battling polio. When our young man's mom talked about the anguish of having to perform the exercises every night, the other mom said, "Yes, we started to do those exercises, but it caused him so much pain we had to stop."

I have no doubt she loved her son. In fact, she loved him so much that it hurt her to see him in pain. But there is a love that goes deeper than hurting when others hurt—it's the kind of love that allows those we love to be in pain so they can become the kind of people God has designed them to be.

Oh, how I am like that second mom. I hate to see anyone in pain, so I will do whatever I can to protect and comfort those I love—even if it means they stop growing and healing.

Even before we got married, Roger had talked about his dream to take our entire family to Disney World. Roger grew up in Florida, and Disney was a big part of his life. He and his kids hadn't been in over ten years, and my kids had never gone. Two years before Roger's fiftieth birthday, he and I started to make plans for the big trip.

As we started to talk and plan and pray about the trip, I grew more nervous. Our family had traveled together several times before, and it hadn't always been a smooth ride.

- Jeremy, who loves his sister Amanda, can also become very irritated by her. She has a Tigger personality while Jer is more of a laid-back Pooh Bear. Jeremy's irritation with her doesn't happen often, but it can send him into a real funk.

- Kimberly can get her feelings hurt easily, even if no one is giving offense. She has definitely grown in this area, but there are still unknown triggers that can come up and send her into a bad mood.

- My oldest, Justen, hates amusement parks. He would be miserable and would make everyone else miserable at the same time.

- Trying to save money, we were looking for one hotel room for all of us to sleep in. This was causing me to sweat to even think about it.

- In the past, our kids have taken for granted the vacations we've planned and paid for. The sense of entitlement that sometimes accompanied our trips made Roger and me crazy after shelling out all that time and money.

- Roger's extended family, who we love, were going to join us for the trip. It was already becoming obvious that there were a lot of crossed expectations of how we were going to spend our time.

Just planning it was becoming stressful and making our heads spin.

After talking to a lot of parents who had older kids and to our therapist (yes, we're the kind of couple who chats with our therapist before going on vacation), we realized that our plan was to try to make everyone happy, no matter the cost to us.

So we redid vacation—Lipp style. Here are the things we did to stop people-pleasing and start making it a trip we could all enjoy:

We got two hotel rooms. Roger and I realized that we needed space at the end of the day to just be together. So we put the kids in one room, and we stayed in an adjoining room. And it didn't cost us a dime extra, because...

The kids paid for their own room. We'd had this fantasy of giving our kids this trip, but then decided that they would appreciate it more if they contributed to it. A year in advance, we told them that whoever wanted to go, we would expect them to contribute fifty dollars a month toward the trip. Each child ended up contributing a little over five hundred dollars, thereby paying for a hotel room for them to share.

We let our kids off the hook. Justen didn't want to go. The people pleasing/perfectionist part of me wanted to cajole him into coming with us. "You should go. It will be fun! The whole family will be there!" But when we discussed it with him, he just wasn't interested. So we checked in with him periodically, but six months before the trip, we confirmed our plans without Justen. Did it feel weird? Yes. Was it the right thing to do for him and for us? Yes. Justen is an introvert and craves time alone. Having the house to himself was the best vacation we could have given him.

The kids helped us plan. We had a couple of planning meetings in advance to go over such things as budgets and activities. They understood that we weren't using a credit card for this trip, so everything needed to be paid for with cash. We decided as a group to eat breakfast in our room, saving our money instead for a couple of nice dinners at the Animal Lodge and at Be Our Guest (the castle from Beauty and the Beast). We all went into the trip with similar expectations, and it wasn't up to Roger and me to make sure everyone had a magical time.

We talked with our kids before we left about expectations. We told each child that we wanted them to have a good time, but that was going to be 90 percent up to them. If they were upset with someone in the family, it was up to them to talk it out. If they were tired, it was up to them to go back to the room and rest. All the kids were between twenty-one and twenty-six when this trip happened—still kids in a lot of ways, but needing to take responsibility for their own emotional and physical health.

We set expectations with our extended family. Trying to navigate Disney World with a party of fourteen would just be too much. So we set aside one day for all of us to be together and one day for Roger to spend some one-on-one time with his mom. Setting the expectations early was key so that no one was disappointed. Or if they were, at least they were disappointed early and had time to process it.

So, how did all our communication, expressed expectations, and planning go?

While not everything went perfectly, it was the best trip we've ever taken as a family. Yes, we missed Justen, but everyone got along, respected each other's boundaries, and took care of each other. We've never had so many thank-yous from our kids for any trip, and it was a real blessing spending time with them. Our hard choice of giving up people-pleasing led to a great experience for all.

So How Do I Change It?

When we're given the opportunity to people-please, we need to ask ourselves two questions:

1. Is this the best solution for them?
2. Is this the best solution for me?

Here is an example of what I'm talking about:

One of your twentyish kids comes to you and asks for money for a car repair. The problem? The child has no money saved up from their job, and you've loaned this child money before, and it took much longer than promised to get paid back (if at all).

I love a short-term solution. I want everyone to be happy and love me at the end. So my reflex is to help this child out one more time and then insist that they save up money for the next unexpected expense.

Changing the Way I Talk to Myself

I need to change the dialogue I have with myself when it comes to situations like this. Instead of, "What will she think of me if I don't give her the money?" I need to ask myself:

1. Is this the best solution for them?

"No, because if I solve this for him now, he won't learn how to solve it for himself in the future."

"No. She is only respectful when she wants something. She is learning how to manipulate people."

"No. I'm teaching her that she doesn't have to save for emergencies. I will always be there when she falls down."

I know. Your mommy heart is going to bleed.

How will she get to school? How will he get to work? These are things your child needs to figure out. If they chose not to save up for emergencies, then they need to have a backup plan. You cannot be that all-encompassing backup plan. Like one of our survey takers said, you are crippling your kids when you are their go-to plan.

2. Is this the best solution for me?

Even if you can convince yourself that it is the best plan for you to provide the money to your child, you can't convince me that it's the best plan. If that child didn't keep to the terms of your last agreement, you have to take the attitude, "Fool me once, shame on you. Fool me twice, shame on me."

When I've been in this circumstance before, my initial guilt was released by the supposed loan. However, bitterness and resentment built up when my child didn't keep up their end of the bargain. Especially when I saw them spending money on clothes, eating out, and other non-essentials. That's not how I want to feel about my kids.

Changing the Way I Talk to Others

I had to give myself new scripts when it came to talking with others and setting boundaries. Yes, it's hard. But if you are in this relationship and your goal is long-term peace, not just a short-term fix, you need to be clear with those you love.

Here is what I had to say to my child who wanted to borrow money:

"You know I love you more than just about anything on the planet, so I want to be honest with you about how I feel. I'm not comfortable with lending you money anymore. Over the past few years, when money issues have come up, I've felt like I've been there for you, but you didn't keep up your end of the bargain.

"I know this may sound harsh, but I want to have a great relationship with you, and I can't when I feel bitterness.

"I can and will help you in other ways. I will help you navigate the best place to get your car repaired, and I can help you for three days getting to school and work. But I cannot lend you money."

Did my child understand? No. Did they punish me with their silence and moody attitude for days to come? Yes. But I gathered a few friends around me to hold me accountable, and I did the right thing for me and my child.

It's a brave woman who risks being disliked in the short-term in order to experience—and share—healthy living with those around her. Let's be brave together.

Tiny Acts of Rebellion

1. I will resist the urge to smooth over an argument between my kids.

2. I will tell my friend where I'd like to meet for lunch instead of saying, "Wherever you want to go is fine with me."

3. I will tell my boss that I can't work late on a night I have plans with my friends.

4. I will view my kids' trials as character building, and not something that needs to be avoided at all costs.

Tips for Each Rebel Type

Expressive

You love being happy and want everyone else to be happy too. You'll often do whatever it takes to entertain, be cute, and make others laugh, regardless of what you may actually be feeling. Guard against letting others take advantage of your need for attention and approval. Some people will withhold their happiness just to see how much they can get out of you, which isn't healthy for anyone involved. Remember: the only person's happiness you're responsible for is your own.

Analytic

You genuinely want to contribute to others' happiness. But since happiness is not your personal measurement of victory, you often have trouble knowing how to do so. For example, you may correct how someone pronounces a word with the belief that they could not possibly be happy being wrong. Since being right is what gives you satisfaction, you assume it makes others happy too. Pay attention to how others respond to your corrections and other attempts to be helpful. If they don't seem pleased, try something else.

Driver

You tend to have a "deal with it and move on" philosophy. Of all the personalities, you are the least likely to cave in to this bully belief. You see others' happiness as their problem, not yours. "Not my circus, not my monkeys" is one of your many mottos. If someone close to you is unhappy, you may give one shot at cheering them up so you can say, "Well, at least I tried." Although you are not responsible for others' happiness, being more aware of your impact on them will serve you well.

Amiable

You tend to feel responsible for every sigh, every frown, and every look of boredom, but you don't know exactly what to do about them. The more unhappy others seem, the worse you're likely to feel, causing you to disappear in a cloud of shame. One of your greatest challenges is learning to allow others to have their emotions without you absorbing and feeling responsible for them. You are responsible for yourself, first and foremost.

CHAPTER 16

What You Do Does Not Equal Who You Are

Refuse to be defined by the St. Patrick's Day cupcakes
you take to your kid's class.

✳

*"Since I grew up in a home where I felt I had to justify
my space on this earth by doing things, I've slipped
into that mode far more than I wish to admit."*

MARY DEMUTH, *Beautiful Battle*

> **Bully belief 8:** "I am what I do."

"I'm just so overwhelmed!" I (Cheri) told my principal.

My second year of teaching started out exhilarating but soon became exhausting. I spent eight hours a day with my lively seventh and eighth graders. My class had twenty-one boys and seven girls—who made up for their low quantity with high intensity.

I had seven lessons to plan and teach each day, followed by all the grading. I arrived at school early each morning and stayed late each evening. I wanted to be known as an on-top-of-it teacher.

I'd bought a new computer for the classroom and was trying to figure out how to use it (this was back in the day of C prompts). I wanted to be seen as a tech-savvy teacher.

I ran a drama ministry group after school and on weekends. We were planning a big performance for our upcoming parent-student banquet. I wanted to be a fun and popular teacher.

Plus I was in the second trimester of my first pregnancy. So I was working on all the things I needed to do in order to be a good mother. While, of course, still doing good wife stuff.

Hoping for sympathy, and perhaps a few days off, I vented to my principal. She listened sympathetically and then made a blunt observation: "Yes, Cheri, you sure did all this to yourself, didn't you."

After the shock of wounded pride wore off, I realized she was right. In my drive to do enough, I had done all this to myself. And so much more.

At home, I stayed up late sewing custom maternity outfits so that I'd be a cute preggie. On weekends, I took our Samoyed dog to shows, aiming to champion her so we could breed her. At church, I taught the juniors, since that seemed like something a good pastor's wife would do.

Why? I did all this to myself so that...

- my students' parents would think I was a good teacher
- my boss would be impressed
- church members would consider me an asset to my husband
- people would compliment me
- I would finally feel like I was enough

Trying Hard So That...

To see how much the belief "I am what I do" is influencing you, rank each statement and total up your answers at the end.

Strongly **1** Disagree	Disagree **2**	Neutral **3**	Agree **4**	Strongly **5** Agree

1. I live by my lists. I can't imagine a life without lists!

  1 2 3 4 5

2. I feel like I have to prove my worth through my achievements.

  1 2 3 4 5

3. Interruptions and unexpected delays frustrate me.

  1 2 3 4 5

4. Sometimes my to-do lists become so long and so detailed that they overwhelm me.

    1   2   3   4   5

5. I get an adrenaline rush when I cross something off my list. (In fact, when I do something that wasn't originally on my to-do list, I write it in just so I can cross it off.)

    1   2   3   4   5

6. I constantly compare myself to others.

    1   2   3   4   5

7. I don't really get the phrase "doing nothing." By definition, *nothing* isn't *doing*.

    1   2   3   4   5

8. I make self-care (rest, nutrition, exercise, regular check-ups) as high a priority as caring for other people in my life.

    1   2   3   4   5

9. I'm a multitasker.

    1   2   3   4   5

10. I can't just sit still and watch a movie. I have to have something in my hands to keep them busy or I have to get up to do things.

    1   2   3   4   5

11. My schedule is typically full with little or no margin for unexpected events or emergencies.

    1   2   3   4   5

12. I get a thrill from starting new projects.

    1   2   3   4   5

13. I sometimes approach personal relationships like projects, with a "checklist mentality."

    1   2   3   4   5

14. I really wouldn't know what to do with downtime or free time.

    1   2   3   4   5

15. I need recognition for my achievements.

    1   2   3   4   5

16. I get more accomplished than most people (and two to three times as much as many).

    1   2   3   4   5

17. Some people are intimidated by me.

    1   2   3   4   5

18. Sometimes I get so focused on projects that I forget about people.

    1   2   3   4   5

19. I often mentally rehearse the tasks I need to do (and the order I need to do them in).

    1   2   3   4   5

20. When I relax, I feel guilty.

    1   2   3   4   5

21. I have a hard time knowing when I've done enough.

    1   2   3   4   5

22. When I'm not accomplishing new things, I feel like a failure.

    1   2   3   4   5

23. I often think, *When this project is done, things will finally get back to normal.*

    1   2   3   4   5

24. When I make a mistake, I feel horrified—as if I am a mistake.

    1   2   3   4   5

25. Key people in my life wish I would spend more time with them.

    1   2   3   4   5

26. I sometimes feel more like a "human doing" than a "human being."

    1   2   3   4   5

27. I skipped bully beliefs 5 ("No fun until my work is done") and 6 ("I'll rest when I'm dead") because I already know I'm too busy to have fun or rest.

    Yes   No   Prefer not to answer

A score of 70 or lower indicates a healthy distance between your sense of self and your sense of accomplishment.

71–100 means that much of your identity comes from what you do.

101–130 says that your sense of self-worth is almost entirely defined by your accomplishments.

(And if you answered Yes to 27…keep reading!)

Many of us claim to believe in salvation by grace. But take one look at our to-do lists or calendars and you'll see what we really believe in—doing, doing, and more doing. Why do we do this to ourselves?

In her book *Stressed-Less Living*, Tracie Miles describes adrenaline addicts as "always overwhelmed, pulled in every direction (often by choice), and stressed to the max. They thrive on the need to feel necessary and productive and possess an insatiable sense of urgency and need for accomplishment."[14]

"We wear busyness like a badge of honor," says Dr. Lissa Rankin. "I'm busy, therefore I'm important and valuable, therefore I'm worthy. And if I'm not busy, forget it. I don't matter."[15]

Never Enough

I posted this Pixar movie dialogue to my Facebook page, with the comment, "I'm probably the only person to get teary while watching *Monsters University*. This scene got to me for so many reasons!" Turned out that dozens of my friends had the same reaction.

Sully: This is all my fault. I'm sorry.

Mike: You were right. They weren't scared of me. I did everything right. I wanted it more than anyone. And I thought…
I thought if I wanted it enough, I could show everybody
that Mike Wizowski is something special. But I'm just…not.

Sully: Look, Mike, I know how you feel.

Mike: Don't do that. Please don't do that. You do not know
how I feel.

Sully: Mike, calm down.

Mike: Monsters like you have everything. You don't have
to be good. You can mess up over and over again, and the
whole world loves you.

Sully: Mike.

Mike: You'll never know what it's like to fail because you
were born a Sullivan!

Sully: Yeah, I'm a Sullivan. I'm the Sullivan who flunked
every test. The one who got kicked out of the program. The
one who's so afraid to let everyone down that I cheated. And
I lied. Mike, I'll never know how you feel. But you're not
the only failure here. I act scary, Mike, but most of the time?
I'm terrified.

Mike: How come you never told me that before?

Sully: Because…we weren't friends before.[16]

Perhaps you identify with Mike. You've believed that if you just tried
hard enough, did everything right, and wanted it bad enough, you'd
arrive. You'd finally achieve the one performance that would prove, once
and for all, that you're special. Worthy. Enough.

Or maybe you understand Sully. You feel like you've spun plates, jug-
gled knives, and swallowed fire trying not to let anyone down. But in
spite of all you do, you still feel like a failure. Sometimes, you're terrified
that you'll never ever be enough.

One Rebel's Story

I was working on my computer when my daughter came to my side. At first she just whined about something random. I shooed her away, *as this was clearly interfering with very important email.*

She approached on the other side, and her whining picked up momentum. I took a quick glance: *no blood, no contusions.* So I tried to ignore her and focus on the email I *had* to send.

A few moments passed and then the tears started. Big tears. Not just little dangling tears threatening to fall, but actual real tears falling from her eyes. She buried her head into her folded arms right on top of my desk. I had to stop what I was doing because her hair was blocking my keyboard.

"What is wrong?" I asked impatiently. I got no verbal response, only big, heavy, four-year-old sobs.

"Seriously, what is wrong? Did your brother do something to you? Are you hurt? Are you bleeding? Do you need help with something?" Nothing but sniffles, as she dug her face deeper into the sleeves of her sweatshirt.

"So what is wrong? Stop for a second. Look at me. Why are you crying?"

She looked up. Her squished red nose was running and she stared at me with big watery eyes in desperation.

"I. DON'T. KNOW!" Her eyes went wide with confusion, then she threw her face back down into her tiny arms. Her shoulders shook as she huddled next to me.

My poor baby. She was just a little girl trying to figure out how to exist in that very moment with feelings she didn't understand, and I wasn't present for her because I had to send an email.

Andé Peña

"Everything I Ever Did"

If you were to write a book about your entire life, how many pages would it have? Hundreds, perhaps? Maybe even thousands?

What if I asked you to summarize everything you've ever done in just one sentence. Could you do it?

The woman Jesus meets at Jacob's well can. After having a deep theological discussion with Jesus, she leaves her jar at the well, goes back to town, and tells everyone, "Come, see a man who told me everything I ever did. Could this be the Messiah?" (John 4:28-29).

"...everything I ever did."

Everything?

Exactly what has Jesus said about her past? "The fact is, you have had five husbands, and the man you now have is not your husband" (John 4:18).

That's it. One sentence. Her account of "everything I ever did" is a list of relationship failures. She has failed so many times, she considers herself a failure.

This is the danger of believing "I am what I do": when I fail, I become a failure. And since I fail all the time, the bullies convince me to spend my life believing that I am a failure. All the time.

But notice the transformation in the woman as a result of her time with Jesus.

First, she leaves her jar at the well. Maybe she's so excited that she forgets what she's doing. Or perhaps she knows she can't run fast enough with the jar. Either way, she's bursting to tell others about Jesus!

Then, she tells people to come see Jesus. They do, and after spending time with him, they no longer believe just because of her testimony. They believe because they've seen and heard for themselves and "know that this man really is the Savior of the world" (John 4:42).

If you're living under the bully belief "I am what I do," you may feel defined by your failures. Or perhaps you feel defined by your latest success, which you're desperately trying to keep from fading into a failure. Either way, God offers you a very different *identity*. He invites you to become:

1. A woman who encounters Jesus. We have an open invitation to spend time with him. Any time. To ask him questions and listen to his answers. Encounter him often.

2. A woman who leaves her jar at the well. Not a literal jar, of course, but we all lug our agendas to the well. Agendas overflowing with ways we try to meet our own needs. Agendas so heavy we stagger under each step. Agendas brimming with plans for trying hard "so that..." Leave your agenda with Jesus.

3. A woman who invites others to know Jesus. When we've spent time with Jesus and left our agendas with him, the most natural response will be to invite others to "Come see!" So they can hear him for themselves. So they will know that he is the Savior of the world. Invite others to find what you've found.

How to Break the Busyness Addiction

One of the most convicting lines I've ever read in a blog post was written by my friend Sandi Brewer: "[God] wanted me to realize that I cannot do everything, be everything, experience everything, and have everything; that is greedy."[17]

That's right: trying to "do it all" is a form of greed. These five tools can help you leave behind do-it-all greed as you follow where God leads:

1. Ask, "Am I Being Driven or Led?"

Bully-driven thinking sounds a lot like this: "I have to _____ so that..."

- my husband will be happy with me.
- my clients will respect me.
- I will feel better about myself.

When you do a task "so that," it's a sure sign that you're being driven. Spirit-led thinking goes: "I'm choosing to _____ because..."

- I am already loved by God.
- God calls me his masterpiece.
- Jesus gave his life, and I am a new person with a new life!

You do tasks "because" when you're being led. You're not striving to find your identity in accomplishments. Rather, you're living out the unique identity God's given you.

2. Ask, "Am I Focused on the Product or the Process?"

Kathi and I attended the She Speaks Intensive training through Proverbs 31 Ministries in January 2013. Our motto was "The process is the point," and I've been repeating it ever since. I remind myself, "The process is the point" when

- I start feeling envious of someone else's latest success.
- I wish my goals didn't feel so far away.
- I resent working so hard.
- I start trying to force results.
- I feel like giving up.

It's not that results are unimportant. They just shouldn't be our primary focus. A strong process will naturally produce strong outcomes.

In *A Million Miles in a Thousand Years* Donald Miller makes a similar point. Our destination doesn't shape who we become; it's the journey that transforms us.[18]

Jaroldeen Asplund Edwards, who planted her famed daffodil garden over a span of forty years, put it this way: "One bulb at a time. There was no other way to do it. No shortcuts—simply loving the slow process of planting. Loving the work as it unfolded. Loving an achievement that grew slowly and bloomed for only three weeks each year."[19]

3. Make Your To-Do List Work for You

In *The Get Yourself Organized Project*, Kathi recommends creating two kinds of to-do lists: the Master List and the daily To-Do List.[20]

On the Master List, you put "absolutely everything you need to get done in life." Under each item, create a list of "Next Steps." The purpose of your Master List is to make sure you don't forget anything (or stay up all night worrying that you might have).

The daily To-Do List holds Next Steps but no Master List items (unless they're short 'n' sweet). The To-Do list goes everywhere with you.

The Master List keeps track of the end products while the daily To-Do List keeps you focused on the process, moving forward one step at a time.

4. Make a "Ta-Da!" List

Keep track of small milestones along the way and celebrate them! You might do this via Facebook or in a scrapbook or even a simple list on your fridge. If you achieve some big results, by all means enjoy them. But focus on what's within your control: your choices to take those Next Steps.

5. Decide when Enough Is Enough

Some of us have a hard time knowing when our work is done. Nobody ever tells us, "You've done enough! Stop working and go home."

Other people will always take whatever you give them, and many will request even more. There will always be more work you could be doing. You have to define *enough* for yourself. Then you have to defend your enough decision. Here's what this might look like in action:

1. Commit to yourself, "I'll work on this for thirty minutes; that will be enough."

2. Set a timer for thirty minutes and work.

3. When the timer goes off, stop working.

That's it. Of course, it's the "defend" part that's hard. The timer rings and you think, *Just ten more minutes.* Before you know it, an hour has passed, and your enough decision has gone undefended.

Decide. Do. Defend.

It's up to you.

"Do Less but Accomplish More"

The *Jesus Calling* devotional reminds us, "Doing countless unnecessary activities will dissipate your energy. When you spend time with Me, I restore your sense of direction. As you look to Me for guidance, I enable you to do less but accomplish more."[21]

Does the idea of doing less but accomplishing more make you want to wave your hand and yell, "Pick me! Pick me!"?

He already has. We're the ones who need to pick him, not the other way around. We're the ones who need to remember to "be still" so that we can know he is God (and we are not).

As you stop trying harder to do enough, you'll start being still with him. You'll make the braver choice to leave your agenda with him. To leave your fears with him. To move forward in his love.

You'll remember that the process is the point. And you'll remember to let him lead.

Tiny Acts of Rebellion

1. I will get a timer specifically for timing "enough."

2. I will multitask with tasks but not with people.

3. I will post on my mirror a sign that says, "The process is the point!"

4. I will think of a creative way to introduce myself that does not make my job my identity.

5. I will celebrate even the smallest "Ta-Da" moments.

Tips for Each Rebel Type

Expressive

Your focus on your social accomplishments can cause this bully belief to snare. When your social media pages are "liked" or you get invited to important parties, you feel worthwhile. When people aren't paying attention to you, you feel lost. The end of an important relationship can throw you for a tailspin if you're not careful. Remember: your identity is always in Christ, not other flawed fickle humans. You are loved without reservation, no matter what the THL bullies say.

Analytic

Perfectionism customizes this bully belief just for you— "I am *how* I do things"—so you'll be more likely to agree with its premise. The implication is that if you do things perfectly, you must be perfect. This sets you up to view everything you do as a reflection of your identity and worth: your home, your car, your clothes, your parenting, your marriage, your job, and so on. While aiming for excellence is one of your assets, beware of the temptation to stray to extremes, especially in your relationships.

Driver

Of all the personalities, you're the most likely to defend this bully belief. After all, the Bible says that faith without works is dead, right? And Jesus said, "You will know them by their fruits," right? When the THL bullies get ahold of you, it takes very little persuading for you to agree that the more you produce, the more valuable you are. The longer your to-do list and the more items checked off, the greater your worth. Don't buy into the belief that you are nothing more than a human doing; remember that you are a human being, created and dearly loved by God.

Amiable

You naturally focus more on who others are than what they do. You're intuitively aware that while people can "fake it 'til you make it" externally, their hearts cannot. You align with 1 Samuel 16:7: "People look at the outward appearance, but the LORD looks at the heart." The extreme you want to watch for is an attitude that actions and achievements are irrelevant, failing to see that who you are is ultimately expressed in what you do (or don't do).

CHAPTER 17

Enough Really Is Enough

How to stop keeping three dozen empty egg cartons just in case.

✳

"When you're clear about your purpose and your priorities, you can painlessly discard whatever does not support these, whether it's clutter in your cabinets or commitments on your calendar."

VICTORIA MORAN, *Lit from Within*

Bully belief 9: "I can't throw it away; I might need it someday!"

Grandma always stowed hardboiled eggs in her purse when she flew from Michigan to California to visit. She'd pull out a couple of eggs shortly after takeoff, crack them open, and nibble away. Hunching over her purse, she tried to hide what she was doing. But her tiny frame was no shield against the sulfurous fumes that wafted through the cabin. Before and after the midflight meal, she'd pull out a couple of eggs again. Shortly before landing, two more.

As a child in Germany during World War I, Grandma had experienced food shortages and hunger. As a result, she always carried food with her "just in case." When leaving a buffet restaurant, she stuffed her purse with apples. After a church potluck, she filled her pockets with napkin-wrapped rolls and brownies. Grandma didn't pack food with her because she was hungry. She didn't carry it because she feared an immediate food shortage. She kept it handy as insurance that she would never go hungry again.

Since she never took more than she could carry with her, Grandma's food hoarding habit seemed like a harmless quirk. But as I (Cheri) have started to recognize the "hard-boiled eggs" I've stuffed throughout my life—in my home, my garage, my schedule, my mind, and my heart—I'm seeing that my own "just in case" habits are anything but harmless.

I've spent years asking myself two questions that I thought were unrelated.

The first question, "Why do I still have this?" I asked several times per day as I noticed unused gadgets in the kitchen, looked at unworn outfits in my closet, and stumbled over that same stack of boxes in the garage.

The second question, "Why do I feel so stuck?" I asked whenever I tried to make progress with a new project or finally finish up an old one that I'd started weeks, months, even years ago.

I finally realized that the answer to the second question could be found in the answers to the first: I was feeling stuck because of all my unnecessary stuff. My stuff was holding me back. So I got serious about answering, "Why do I still have this?" At first, I just focused on physical belongings; but I soon expanded to include my schedule, my habits, and my beliefs.

Holding On for Dear Life

How stuffed with "just in case" clutter is your life? Circle Yes or No to each question and then total up your Yes answers.

1. Yes No   I frequently look at things I own and ask myself, "Why do I still have this?"

2. Yes No   I often feel guilty for spending money on items I don't use.

3. Yes No   I have some habits that were helpful once but are now getting in my way.

4. Yes No   I own quite a few things that I have not used in six months or more.

5. Yes No   I hold on to a number of beliefs that may be downright destructive.

6. Yes No   I buy things I don't really need just because they're on sale.

7. Yes No   I keep things I don't need or want because someone I care about gave them to me.

8. Yes No   I constantly wish I had more time.

9. Yes No   I have a hard time forgiving other people who have offended me.

10. Yes No   I tend to expect a lot of myself.

11. Yes No   My house or garage is full of stuff.

12. Yes No   When I don't have money in the bank but see something I want, I often pull out my credit card and just charge it.

13. Yes No   I have a junk drawer or junk room.

14. Yes No   I dread the thought of moving because we have so much stuff that I'd have to sort and pack.

15. Yes No   I sort through our stuff and give some of it away regularly, but somehow we never seem to have any less.

16. Yes No   We have things that we don't use, but we keep them "just in case."

17. Yes No   I'm ashamed to have people over to my house because it's so cluttered and messy.

18. Yes No   I tend to hold grudges.

19. Yes No   I have collections that require a lot of space to store or display.

20. Yes No   I have high expectations for other people in my life.

If you circled more than five Yes answers, clutter may be taking control of your life. This chapter will help you take back control from your clutter, both physical and emotional.

How do we end up with so much stuff in the first place? And then hold on to it as if our lives depended on it? As I've been unstuffing my life, I've discovered dozens of well-intentioned reasons. Here are three biggies:

1. We Buy in Hopes of Becoming

Let's go into my kitchen, open a drawer, and pull out the first unused item we can find. Ahhhh, a Pampered Chef ice cream cookie sandwich maker, NIB (that's an eBay acronym for "new in box"). I'm pretty sure I bought it six years ago at a Pampered Chef party. I went just to support the hostess and socialize; I dislike cooking and avoid it as much as possible.

But while the demonstrator was showing off her gadgets, I saw a vision. A vision of the kind of woman I could become, if only I owned whatever she was showing at the time. That evening, I decided, "Yes, I want to become the kind of woman who makes ice cream cookie sandwiches for her children!"

So I bought the gadget. I bought the gadget that would help me become the kind of woman I wanted to be. But I never became that woman. I only bought into the illusion that having the right equipment would transform me into that woman.

You may not have a Pampered Chef ice cream cookie sandwich maker in your kitchen drawer. But I'm guessing you have at least one or two things you've purchased with high hopes of personal transformation.

It's so tempting to buy in order to become. Too often, though, we only buy. We never become.

2. We Try to Recoup Our Financial Losses

Now let's head out to my garage. See those four big boxes full of dusty Breyer model horses? I've had some of those since I was five years old. (That's four dec…a very long time ago.) We've carted those boxes through four moves. Why? Because I remember paying twenty to thirty dollars each for some of them, and I know that a bunch of them (okay, at least one) used to be worth almost a hundred dollars.

Are they worth that much now? Well, not the last time I checked. But you never know when the not-so-gently-used model horse market could have a sudden jump in value.

We hold on to things like model horses in an attempt to hold on to the money they represent. But the original money is long gone. In my case, the models that were once worth anything have long since lost all value due to damage.

And yet, we hold on.

3. We Hope the Good Old Days Will Return

Back in the house to my scrapbooking room. Yes, room. Can you believe all these supplies? Paper and cardstock and albums and refill pages and punches and die cuts and embellishments and pens and storage cases and totes and rolling drawer carts for everything.

When was the last time I scrapped? Hmmm…must be about nine years ago. Why haven't I done anything since then? Well, now that you mention it, I'm actually not much of a scrapbooker. I loved going to crops with my daughter and a few friends when we lived in southern California. I'd do a few pages, but mostly I talked and ate and ate and talked.

After moving, I faithfully hung on to my supplies and even kept buying more. But after all these years, it turns out I'm more of a scrapbooking supply collector than anything else.

It's so easy to keep holding on to supplies so we'll be ready when our lives go back to the way things used to be.

But they don't.

Stuffing vs. Stewarding

So are you ready to scold me for all my failures?

I didn't think so.

You may be shaking your head and thinking I'm a bit nuts. But I'll bet you're also chuckling because you understand, to some degree, why I've hung on to my Pampered Chef ice cream sandwich cookie maker, my model horses, and my scrapping supplies for so long.

Will you promise to extend this same grace to yourself throughout this chapter? If I'm not a failure, then you're not either. We're both dearly beloved daughters of God's delight. We've been beat up by bullies for long enough; let's agree not to beat up on ourselves.

Deal?

Okay, here's the deal: When it comes to figuring out if we're stuffing our lives or stewarding what God's given to us, we can ask two key questions.

1. Does this feed my insecurity or uphold my integrity?

When the thought of letting go makes me cling all the tighter, I'm holding on out of insecurity. My identity is at stake. I'm wondering, "Who will I be without this?"

Integrity, however, raises the question, "Does keeping this match my identity?" I know who I am in Christ. When I choose to keep belongings, commitments, habits, and beliefs that are consistent with who I am, and let go of those that are not, that's integrity.

2. Does this fuel compulsion or contribution?

A sure sign that I'm trapped in compulsion is the need to keep things all to myself. Compulsion is always based on a self-centered scarcity mentality. The bullies fill me with fears that I'll never have another chance or that I'll regret this forever if I let go. Whatever I have, I must keep; and then I must keep accumulating to safeguard my stash.

Contribution, on the other hand, works from an abundance mindset. God's many gifts are meant to be enjoyed and shared. Whatever I have should actively enhance my well-being and growth. And I should use whatever I have to actively contribute to the well-being and growth of others.

Stewardship is only holding on to things that uphold integrity and fuel contribution. Stuffing is clinging to things that feed insecurity and fuel compulsion.

One Rebel's Story

It was like a bad episode of *Hoarders*. Closets full of old, overused items, hidden away "in case I need it someday." Bins of jeans two sizes two big (or too small) because one day I may magically gain (or lose) fifteen pounds in a week, and I'll grab them to remedy my sudden jeans emergency.

For most of my young adulthood, I hoarded everything. Although I kept my possessions neatly tucked away in organized bins, I still had issues with letting go of my stuff. Because deep down, my *physical* stuff represented all the *emotional* stuff I refused to let go of. I refused to give up on the things that meant the most to me because I was afraid that God wouldn't provide for me what I needed when I needed it.

But then one day God asked me a question I'll never forget: *"Why don't you come to me with your needs?"*

I thought that I did, but instead I doubted. I doubted God, his provision, and ultimately, his love.

Michelle Lazurek

God Asks Us to Let Go

Sometimes we feel convicted to let things go but can't bear the thought. We wonder, *Why can't I just hold on? How bad would it be to keep it? What's wrong with a bit of extra stuff?* Let's look at these three questions from a biblical perspective.

Why Can't I Just Hold On?

God makes it clear in Ecclesiastes 3:

> There is a time for everything,
> and a season for every activity under the heavens…
> a time to search and *a time to give up,*
> a time to keep and *a time to throw away.*
> (3:1,6)

How Bad Would It Be to Keep It?

When God provided manna to the children of Israel, he told them to gather only what they needed for the day.

> Then Moses said to them, "No one is to keep any of it until morning." However, some of them paid no attention to Moses; they kept part of it until morning, but it was full of maggots and began to smell (Exodus 16:19-20).

When God asks us to let something go, we won't be able to keep it. Oh, we may hold on to it, but it will spoil, one way or another.

What's Wrong with a Bit of Extra Stuff?

Tucked in Jesus's vine-and-branches metaphor is a vital detail that's easy to overlook:

> "I am the true vine, and my Father is the gardener. He cuts off every branch in me that bears no fruit, while every branch that does bear fruit he prunes so that it will be even more fruitful" (John 15:1-2).

Did you catch it? Jesus said that the gardener (God) prunes the branches that do bear fruit (us) *so that they will produce even more fruit.*

If we don't let God de-clutter us, we'll miss out on the amazing new growth opportunities he has planned for us.

What to Give Up

Remember a time, perhaps a Thanksgiving dinner, when you ate so much you became uncomfortably full. Perhaps you were even in pain for an hour or two.

Now recall a time when you hadn't eaten for so long that you were famished. Your blood sugar dropped so low you were trembling. All you could think of was finding some food.

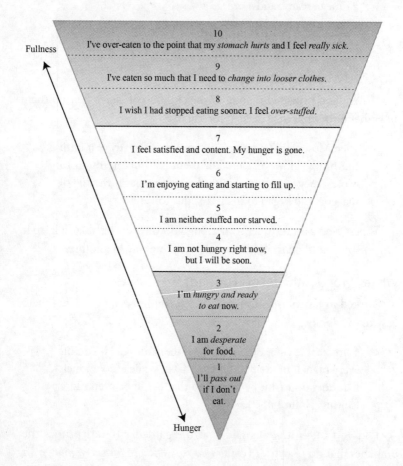

Fullness

10
I've over-eaten to the point that my *stomach hurts* and I feel *really sick.*

9
I've eaten so much that I need to *change into looser clothes.*

8
I wish I had stopped eating sooner. I feel *over-stuffed.*

7
I feel satisfied and content. My hunger is gone.

6
I'm enjoying eating and starting to fill up.

5
I am neither stuffed nor starved.

4
I am not hungry right now, but I will be soon.

3
I'm *hungry and ready to eat* now.

2
I am *desperate* for food.

1
I'll *pass out* if I don't eat.

Hunger

We're going to use this fullness-hunger spectrum as a tool to evaluate our "fullness" and "hunger" levels in all areas of our lives. Looking at the middle of the spectrum, four through seven, you see words like *enjoying*, *satisfied*, and *content*. When your physical belongings, your schedule, your habits, and your beliefs nurture these feelings, they are in the healthy range of "enough."

Overstuffed Areas of Your Life

By looking at the top and bottom of the spectrum, you can find answers to the question, "What should I give up?" At the top of the fullness scale, you see words like *overstuffed* and *sick*. To find which areas of your life are overstuffed, finish these statements:

"I have so many commitments on my calendar that_____
_____."

(Examples: *"I rarely see my husband"* or *"I'm too busy when my kids have an emergency."*)

"I have so much stuff in my house/garage that_____
_____."

(Examples: *"I never invite anyone over for dinner"* or *"we park the car in the driveway."*)

"I have so many expectations for myself/others that_____
_____."

(Examples: *"I'm constantly disappointed in myself"* or *"I'm always irritated at people I love."*)

Areas of your life in which you have "too much" are the places to start giving up.

Starving Areas of Your Life

On the bottom of the hunger spectrum, you see words like *hungry* and *desperate*. To find which areas of your life are being starved, finish these statements:

"With freed-up time, I could_____
_____."

(Examples: *"have some personal quiet time each day"* or *"do something I've been sensing God calling me to do."*)

*"With more open space, I could*_____

_____ *."*

(Examples: *"enjoy my home as a refuge and sanctuary"* or *"invite people into my home without feeling embarrassed."*)

*"With hope instead of expectations, I could*_____

_____ *."*

(Examples: *"try new things and be okay with making mistakes"* or *"give others the freedom to fail as they learn and grow."*)

You'll be able to start filling in these "not enough" areas of your life as you give up stuff in the areas that have "too much."

Not Too Much, Not Too Little

A year ago, I was given the opportunity to host a girls' Bible study in my home. In the past, I'd never had the time, due to an overfull calendar. I'd refused to have anyone in my house because I was ashamed how packed it was with clutter and dust. And I was stuffed to the gills with insecurity: *I'm too boring. They won't like me. They'll come once and never come back.*

This time, I recognized the bullies at work and chose love over fear. I focused on my lifelong desire to make a difference in the lives of young women. I'd been de-cluttering my house and declared it "good enough." And I decided that the best way to rebel against the bullies was to obey God's call and leave the results up to him.

To my surprise, my girls don't care if boxes are stacked in the entry, that my sofa has spots on it, or whether I'm the perfect discussion leader. As long as my front door is open to them at 6:30 and brownies are hot out of the oven, it's all good. In fact, my new motto is, "Wherever two or three are gathered, Mrs. G will bake brownies."

I have no idea if I'm doing things the right way or not. I'm resisting the urge to ask my girls what they think. When I see their pile of shoes at the front door, I feel *satisfied* and *content*: I feel *enough.*

Who I am is enough because God is more than enough.

Cutting From "Too Much" to Fill In "Not Enough"

It's time to get really practical here. Brainstorm some ways you can unstuff the overfull areas of your life so you can nourish the areas that are starving.

1. I will prayerfully consider giving up [area of too much]_____

    _____

    because I'd like to start [area of not enough] _____

    _____.

2. I will prayerfully consider giving up [area of too much]_____

    _____

    because I'd like to start [area of not enough]_____

    _____.

3. I will prayerfully consider giving up [area of too much]_____

    _____

    because I'd like to start [area of not enough]_____

    _____.

As you move away from the extreme ends of the scale and toward a healthier balance in the middle, you'll start to feel *satisfied* and *content*: you'll feel *enough*. And you'll discover that who you are is enough because God is more than enough.

How to Let Go

Two progressive steps have helped me let go of stuff, events on my schedule, and even decades-old grudges.

1. Push Pause

Put a moratorium on allowing anything new into your life. Don't buy anything new. Don't add any new events to your calendar. Don't pick a new fight. Don't start any new projects.

Put life on hold as much as possible. This will slow the momentum of the ever-growing snowball of stuff in your life, giving you time to look at and evaluate all areas of your life.

You're more likely to look at your calendar with a critical eye if you're not in the middle of justifying why you're adding one more commitment. And you'll be more honest in assessing what needs to stay and what needs to leave your wardrobe if you're not cramming in your three latest bargain buys.

With nothing new entering your life, you can focus on what is already in your life.

2. Commit to One-in-One-Out

You can't bring everything to a standstill for long. But you can decide that as a new thing comes into your life, something old must go to make room for the new.

Before those three bargain buys go into your closet, remove three items that haven't been worn in a long while. When the call comes to bake brownies for a last-minute parent-teacher organization bake sale, ask which is more important: the impromptu bake sale or next week's meeting that's already on your calendar?

Once you've gotten good at one-in-one-out, graduate to one-in-two-out. When you buy a new kitchen gadget, give away two (hint: chuck the ones with the most dust on them). Before taking on a new project, prayerfully consider which two prior commitments to let go.

Let me warn you right up front: one-in-two-out can cause panic. With one-in-one-out, you feel like you're maintaining equilibrium. So even though things are changing, the overall amount of stuff in your life is staying the same. But when you start evicting two old for every one new, fear can rise up. If you're not used to having free time on your calendar, you might fear that you're becoming lazy. If you're not used to having empty space in your closets or cupboards, you may fear scarcity.

These fears are normal. When reducing areas of your life that have been overstuffed for so long, it takes trial and error to figure out the differences between too much, too little, and just right. Change can be scary, and letting go feels like loss. Keep extending yourself grace.

Safe in the Middle

When we find ourselves on either end of the spectrum—stuffed or starved—we can be sure the bullies have driven us there. They've used fear to trap us in the no-win extremes of "too much" and "never enough."

Instead, as we listen to the Holy Spirit, he will guide us to the middle.

In the middle, we will find the elusive thing so many of us have given up on: balance.

In the middle, we will no longer feel the need to stuff or starve ourselves.

In the middle, we will reach the place we've been searching for so long: enough.

When we stop trying harder to have enough, this is where we'll find ourselves: living braver in the middle of God's love.

Tiny Acts of Rebellion

1. I will identify one old habit that I need to let go of.

2. I will spend five minutes de-cluttering one small area of one room.

3. I will select one item I'm not using and give it to someone who I know will enjoy using it.

4. I will keep a wish list instead of buying on impulse something not on my shopping list.

5. I will remember that "sale" still means I'm spending money.

Tips for Each Rebel Type

Expressive

You're so creative that you can look at anything and think, *Oh, I could make a ___ out of this!* or *I could do ___ with that!* But as much as you love your ideas, there's no way you can do them all. You don't need to buy or keep the stuff that goes along with your great ideas. Share your surplus with others who will use it. When it comes to de-cluttering, don't go it alone. Grab a Bravery Buddy to cheer you along and hand you Kleenex as you cry sentimental tears.

Analytic

You share the Boy Scout motto: "Be prepared." You remember with great clarity the time you gave something away and the very next day you needed it, and you're not going to make that mistake twice. Deciding what to keep and what to let go of is difficult because you might make the wrong choice. Don't let fear keep you from starting. De-clutter slowly, a few simple decisions at a time. You'll gain skill and confidence as you go.

Driver

You tend to prefer a streamlined approach to life, and clutter gets in the way. You tend to hang on to anything that keeps your options open, that gives you greater choices. You're less likely than other personalities to hold on to sentimental stuff unless it has practical value. Your "let it go and move on" approach to all of life is an asset. Be patient with other personalities who struggle with hanging on and looking back. They need to learn how to "just get over it" in their own ways; they will appreciate your encouragement and support.

Amiable

Inertia will be one of your biggest struggles when it comes to de-cluttering any area of your life. Sorting and culling involve difficult decisions and even painful memories. Many of your possessions have been given to you by friends and family members, and since you value the people, you feel you must keep the items in order to avoid hurting the people.

CHAPTER 18

No More Last Minute

How to take "I work better under pressure" out of your vocabulary.

✳

"My evil genius Procrastination has whispered
me to tarry 'til a more convenient season."

MARY TODD LINCOLN

> **Bully belief 10:** "I work better under pressure."

If you want to know how close I (Kathi) am to a deadline on a project, all you have to do is look at the state of my house.

I tend to start all of those cleaning tasks about three weeks before a big project is due. Three weeks is long enough to tell my brain that I still have plenty of time to get things done, but short enough that I'm feeling the pressure and want to do something else. I'm about three weeks out from a major deadline and there are no crumbs in my silverware tray, the grout on the kids' bathroom tub is sparkly, and every one of our socks has found its mate or been sent to the great recycling bin in the sky.

"I work better under pressure" was my mom's favorite mantra. She is famous for pulling together miracles at the last minute. Whether it was a costume we needed for school or a quilt she was entering in the state fair, my mom always came through and her handiwork was always amazing. But I didn't realize, until I too was a procrastinating adult, the toll those last-minute projects took on her. I remember hearing her say, "I don't know what's wrong with me! Why do I do everything at the last minute?"

Why We Listen to the Procrastination Bully

Place a checkmark by the following thoughts that you identify with:

1. _____ I thrive on the excitement of a last-minute deadline.

2. _____ I do my best work right before it's due.

3. _____ I'm accomplished at winging it.

4. _____ The work I do at the last possible minute is better than what most people spend weeks working on.

5. _____ I can't get started sooner because I have so many important things to get done first.

6. _____ I have to wait until inspiration strikes.

7. _____ The adrenaline rush of waiting puts me at peak performance.

8. _____ Some of my favorite memories are of the all-nighters I've pulled while part of a team on a tight deadline.

9. _____ I'm smart enough to pull it off at the last minute.

10. _____ I'm not a fan of delayed gratification. I do what feels good first.

11. _____ When I wait until it's a crisis, other people step in and help me or even do it for me.

12. _____ If I end up doing lousy work, I can always save face by saying, "Oh, I threw it together at the last minute."

13. _____ I'm a starter, not a finisher.

14. _____ I'm a free spirit. I don't work well within the confines of schedules and deadlines.

15. _____ I love telling my war stories of how I got an impossible amount done in a short span of time.

16. _____ The closer to the deadline I wait, the less exercise and sleep I get.

17. _____ When I've procrastinated as long as I possibly can, I need a ton of junk food to get me through the actual work.

18. _____ When I suddenly have to devote all my time and energy into meeting a deadline, I get grouchy and snippy with people.

19. _____ Procrastination causes me to suffer from sleep deprivation.

20. _____ I used to think that my procrastination affected only me.

Why, oh why do we do this to ourselves? We know that our delay is only going to hurt us in the end, but we believe the lie that we'll do a better job later on. Here are some of the reasons we let our brains fool us:

Postponing Pain. If I put the task off, I can enjoy more things now and do the painful stuff later.

Buy In. "This report is due tomorrow. You need to get the kids dinner." When we're in crisis mode, everyone rallies around us. When we're just doing our jobs, no one is there to pick up the slack.

Panic Produces. When we panic, we produce. We get things done, we check items off our list. The problem is that we don't do anything well and we sacrifice our health, relationships, and sanity in the name of getting things done.

Ego. Why do you think people start to ask a favor of you by buttering you up? "You are the only one who will get it right." "We need someone with your leadership skills." We love being the go-to person for those to-do tasks. It gives us a tiny thrill to know that the teacher appreciation party won't be the same without our homemade snickerdoodles, that the meeting won't be the same without our input, that your friend's daughter feels comfortable only with you, no one else, as a babysitter.

There's a special feeling that comes from believing I am the only one who can make things happen. But when I do things to feel needed and special, I'm putting my value in other people's hands and not in God's Word, where it belongs.

Excuses. "Procrastinators are self-handicappers: rather than risk failure, they prefer to create conditions that make success impossible."[22] Oh, yikes—does that one stare me in the face. How handy to have a reason, an alibi for not performing how I'd hoped or planned.

Discouragement. While I'm a "stuck in the middle" kinda girl, Cheri is an admitted nonfinisher. Here is what she says about not being able to cross the finish line: "I usually quit right around the 90 percent done mark because I'm tired. Getting to that point took more out of me than I realized it would. I feel persecuted that I still have more to do on something that should be done by now."

One Rebel's Story

In my experience, procrastination is a first-cousin of perfectionism. Procrastination doesn't stop me from *beginning* a project or task. I start lots of things with enthusiasm and excitement. I get the train on the track, but somewhere along the way I start to apply the brakes. *Finishing* is often my Achilles' heel.

In a past job as assistant to a university president, I had a wide variety of responsibilities. This was a Jill-of-all-trades-master-of-none situation. My job was cabinet-level, and I interacted and collaborated with others in the administration on their various projects.

I would make lists, research, seek out best practices, ask questions, fine-tune, edit, create file folders of material, and prepare thorough reports outlining the various options and their plusses and minuses. My mantra was "measure twice, cut once."

Our president (my boss) was a chemical engineer by trade and had a very analytical way of approaching things. He was certainly not opposed to research and planning. But he also had a bias for action.

When he came to the university, there was a ten-year master plan. There had *been* a ten-year master plan for quite some time; a plan that was never implemented. By the time he left (in less than ten years) the plan had been fulfilled.

I learned a lot from him. I remember him coming into my office one day and giving me the following advice: "Sarah, 90 is an A." In other words, don't wait for it to be perfect. "Almost perfect" can still be really good. Aim high, but don't quit.

I still make lists and research and plan. But these days I am doing better about moving forward, beyond procrastination, even when things are not *perfect*.

After all, 90 is an A.

Sarah Hensley

God's Guidance Regarding Procrastination

Be very careful, then, how you live—not as unwise but as wise, making the most of every opportunity, because the days are evil. Therefore do not be foolish, but understand what the Lord's will is (Ephesians 5:15-17).

Do not boast about tomorrow,
    for you do not know what a day may bring.
            (Proverbs 27:1)

I want to live with wisdom. I want to be that wise woman who is not staying up until three in the morning. One of the problems that gets in my way is optimism—I always think the project is going to be easier to do later or my life circumstances will be easier later. And that almost never happens. Schedules don't magically clear up, problems don't spontaneously resolve themselves, and now I've left myself no margin for getting the results I want.

God wants us to look at our day and see the opportunities, moments, and gifts that are presently in front of us, not the hoped for or imagined ones of the future.

Understanding the Procrastination Cycle

Procrastination makes you an offer you can't refuse: "Oh, let me take care of you. I'll make your fear disappear!" And then it stabs you in the back. Ever. So. Slowly.

Notice how it works. And how hard it is to break the cycle.

A. You Say Yes

This is the point of great *confidence*. If you're an Expressive, you do this for the fun. An Analytic may say yes to make sure things are done right. For a Driver, it may be the challenge. For an Amiable, it may be a sincere desire to help.

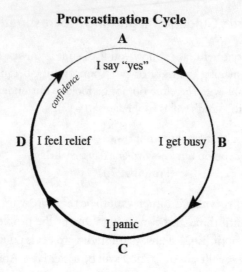

Procrastination Cycle

A — I say "yes"

confidence

D — I feel relief   I get busy — B

I panic

C

B. You Get Busy

For an Expressive, this means she's probably forgetting all about the commitment. An Analytic has it on her calendar, but current projects are taking longer than they should to get just right. The Driver is probably adding more and more to her load because people keep asking, and she keeps volunteering. The Amiable is trying, probably quite successfully, not to think about the commitment at all.

C. You Panic

Anxiety strikes. Suddenly, the deadline looms. You realize you can't possibly fulfill your commitment in the way you agreed to fulfill it. You can't possibly feel the way you had planned to feel about it.

This is where the Expressive may simply call and cancel, often with an elaborate story of how much she wishes she could, how bad she feels about not, and so on. Or she may call in the reinforcements and get a bunch of hardworking friends and family members to rescue her.

The Analytic can't imagine backing out and is likely to do whatever it takes—lost sleep, lack of meals, raging headache—to do what she promised. She's likely to hyper-focus on some details that may not even matter to anyone else, thus all her self-sacrifice will go unnoticed.

A Driver will figure out the bottom line of what absolutely has to be done and plow through it, often leaving a wake of hurt feelings to which she is utterly oblivious. The goal was to get it done, and she got it done. The end.

Our Amiable may disappear altogether. Stop responding to emails. Let the phone ring. Anything to avoid facing anyone until the deadline has actually passed, and it's too late for anything to be done.

D. You Feel Relief

Regardless of personality type, once the deadline has passed, we all feel some form of relief. The Expressive may become extra bubbly and happy. The Analytic may resolve to do better next time. The Driver has moved on. The Amiable is just glad the pressure is off.

The Danger of Relief

The danger of Point D on the Procrastination Cycle is that the feeling of relief gives you a sense of—you guessed it—*confidence*. And where's the point of *confidence* on the cycle?

Oh, back at Point A: You say yes. So instead of truly learning a lesson, you're back where you started. Flooded with adrenaline, determined to have your fun/perfection/achievement/peace, you commit, and the not-so-merry-go-round starts all over again.

How to Break Out of the Procrastination Cycle

No doubt you want your thrills to start coming from being on an all-girl roller derby team, not from driving on the wrong side of the road on April 15 at 11:55 p.m. to get your taxes turned in on time. So how do we start living with some margin in our lives?

Tell a Respected Friend Your Goal

There is something in us procrastinators that wants to save face. That's why sharing your goal for the day with someone you respect is a great way to stop putting off your task. When I'm in the midst of writing a book, I will tell my hubby how many words I'm planning on writing for the day. Because I love Roger and love when he is proud of me, I work hard to achieve my goal. Mind games? Yes. But I get a book and a sense of accomplishment out of it.

Use a Time Box

Parkinson's Law is the adage, "Work expands to fill the time available for its completion." When you have all day to complete a task, it will take you all day to complete that task. If I have three hours to straighten up the house before company comes over, but everything that needs to be done can be done in only thirty minutes, I will suddenly find all those little projects that need to be completed and do them *now*. However, if I set a timer and tell myself "You have only thirty minutes to clean up," I will take those thirty minutes and attack the room and get it clean.

A timer is your best friend if you're a victim of Parkinson's Law. Or if it's a work-related issue, have a set time to work on paperwork (something I'm a master of procrastination at). Two small time boxes—say from 9:00 to 9:30 and 3:00 to 3:30—are better than one big one. Too much time and it's easy to procrastinate within a time box.

Limit Distractions

Checking email is the perfect way to distract you from whatever you're trying to accomplish—it's fast, there may be something interesting in there (definitely more interesting than the mundane task you're working on right now), and you can choose to respond or not depending on your mood (or how badly you don't want to be working on your current project).

Turn off email notifications and shut down that program completely. Close Facebook, Twitter, and Pinterest during your time boxes. Turn the TV off. Not down, off.

Break It Down

I tend to get overwhelmed by the hugeness of projects, and instead of getting started, go watch a *Gilmore Girls* rerun. Instead, when I can objectively break down the project into bite-size pieces (fifteen-minute tasks, for example), I'm not nearly as overwhelmed, and my dread of the project turns to a desire to get some checkmarks toward completion.

Set Up Rewards

There is a place for *Gilmore Girls* reruns—after you've completed part of your task. Break it down, and then when you complete a step, give yourself a break. Looking forward to a break will propel you forward.

Keep a List

I keep a stack of Post-it notes next to my keyboard while I'm working on a project. That way, when I think, "I should check up on our insurance to make sure my last chiropractic visit was reimbursed," I don't have to stop working on my project—I just make a note and move on. I don't fear forgetting my thought, and I can get it done when I have some dedicated web time later on.

If you were to do a quick search of Bible verses about procrastination, you will find a lot of verses with the theme of laziness and slothfulness. But I don't think the problem that most of us have is laziness. I think our problem leans more toward shifting priorities.

We want to attack a project that is before us, but then something comes up—an email that needs to be answered, a problem that needs to be solved, a friend who needs attention. So we drop everything at a moment's notice and tend to the immediate problem instead of the important project.

And let me tell you, sister, that is a never-ending game of Whack-a-Mole.

One of my rules in life (and in my book *The Get Yourself Organized Project*) is to work backward in every situation. Here is an excerpt from that book explaining what "Working Backward" looks like:

> I've spent so much of my life living in reaction mode. This real scene [with my then fourth grader, Justen] is just one example:
> "You need to build a Pentagon out of Popsicle sticks, but it's not due for six weeks? Awesome! I don't have to worry about it for a while."
> *Five weeks and six days later...*
> "What do you mean you have to have a Popsicle Pentagon by tomorrow? AGGGHHH!"
> We all get caught in the occasional crisis. But when you constantly postpone projects and wait until a situation becomes a crisis, that's living in reaction mode. And reaction mode is not a fun way to live.
> That is why I want you to work backward. Look at the questions below and think them through.

- What is your busiest day of the week?
- What is your rest day?
- What day does your garbage and recycling get picked up?
- What is your best day to run errands?
- What is the best day to clean house?

Why am I asking you these questions? Because I want you to work backward.

Let's take the question of "What is your rest day?" For most people, their rest day (if they have one) is Sunday. So if your goal is to rest on Sunday, think about what needs to happen the rest of the week in order for you to rest that day:

- Your work project needs to be done on Friday so you don't have to stress about it Sunday afternoon.
- You need to marinate something in the fridge on Saturday so you can just pop it in the oven on Sunday.
- You need to run errands on Saturday morning.
- Your kids need to be informed that if they need something for a school project, they need to let you know early in the week and not on Sunday evening.

I've determined that the best day for me to clean my house is Tuesday. (And to be perfectly transparent, since I've been working and traveling full-time, I have someone come in twice a month to do the bathrooms, floors, and kitchen.) But it doesn't matter if I'm the one scrubbing floors or it's someone else, there's a lot I need to do to prepare to clean:

- I make sure that each room is picked up.
- I clean out any stray dishes in the sink so that I can scrub the sink.
- I throw away any food that's past its prime so I can clean the fridge.
- I sweep the kitchen and the bathroom.

Since Tuesday is my cleaning day, I do all those above activities before Tuesday so when it's time to clean, nothing is hampering me.

That's what I mean by working backward. It's making an appointment with myself and then working backward to get it done.[23]

It's a counterintuitive way to work, but it assures that not only do the urgent things get done, the important things get done as well. With time to breathe.

And breathing? It's a beautiful thing.

Give yourself the gift of space, time, and breathing. Don't wait until the last minute to take care of yourself.

Tiny Acts of Rebellion

1. I will block off time on my calendar early and often for big projects.
2. I will take care of my future self by not waiting until the last minute.
3. I will ask someone for help when I'm falling behind in a project.
4. I will give myself extravagantly silly rewards for completing tasks early (chocolate and Jane Austin may be involved).

Tips for Each Rebel Type

Expressive

You know how to rally people together to turn last-minute panic into an intense party, with all of us in this together. It combines collaboration, community, and synergy—your favorite things! When the project gets done just in the nick of time, you feel like you've all bonded, as if you've been through an actual battle together. You need to realize that not everyone experiences the same euphoria you do. And while the big picture may be exciting and dazzling, quality may well suffer at the detail level.

Analytic

You know that this bully belief is not actually true for you. So you start early, giving yourself time to do everything right. However, you often get bogged down in less-than-vital details in the early stages and end up lacking momentum to carry you all the way through. Of all the personalities, you are the one most likely to figure out how to break down a large project into baby steps. You're also the most likely to dread group projects because you can't count on others to follow your time-line or quality standards.

Driver

Efficiency is one of your major assets, and it often serves you well. However, you tend not to realize that other people need time—often far more time—to get tasks done. You can't expect everyone to plow through just the way you do. You also can't live on adrenaline. You may say that you thrive on it, but you may be shocked one day when you crash and burn because you've been so out of touch with your body, mind, and spirit.

Amiable

You not only identify with this bully belief, you'd modify it to read, "I start working only when I'm under enough pressure." You may get to the place that you so rarely do anything other than at the last minute that you have no basis of comparison. Try starting a few projects earlier than normal and compare results; you might be in for a surprise. You tend to become easily overwhelmed by large projects. Find a mentor who can help you chop big assignments into small steps that you will do rather than avoid.

CHAPTER 19

Help May Be a Four-Letter Word...
but It's a Good One

Rebels call in reinforcements.

✳

"Asking for help does not mean that we are
weak or incompetent. It usually indicates an
advanced level of honesty and intelligence."

ANNE WILSON SCHAEF

Bully belief 11: "I got myself into this mess, so I have to get myself out."

Back in 2007, I (Kathi) heard about an organization called Overeaters Anonymous (OA). I had already tried every diet on the planet and was once again at that place of desperation. So I turned myself in and started going to meetings three times a week.

OA is in many ways like AA—you keep your abstinence not by refraining from alcohol but by refraining from sugar and flour and adhering to a strict eating schedule, including weighing and measuring everything that goes into your mouth. There is high accountability— you have a sponsor you talk to daily and report all your food to, plus several meetings a week and homework in between.

And it worked. Over the next five months, I lost sixty-six pounds. I was on top of the world.

And then one of my big challenges came: travel. I did fine for most of my trip, until I was at the airport on my way home and was in a panic— I hadn't packed the approved salad dressing.

Every meal had a certain amount and kind of food, and without that dressing, I had messed up my food plan. And since I messed up my food plan, I also lost my abstinence. I was absolutely devastated.

So devastated that I didn't call my sponsor the next day or the day after that. And while I wasn't calling my sponsor, I started down a slippery slope: at first I stopped weighing my food, and then I stopped eating on a schedule. Next, a little bit of flour found its way into my diet, and finally, sugar firmly planted itself in my life.

All the time, I kept thinking, *I will start fresh tomorrow. Once I lose these next few pounds, I will call my sponsor again and start over.*

Can you guess what happened?

Because I didn't ask for help, I kept slipping further and further away from my goal. In less than four months, I'd gained all my weight back (and a couple extra pounds for good measure).

I think back to that time—what if I'd called my sponsor and said, "I blew it. I need to start my program over." I know that my sponsor would have moved heaven and earth to help me. But instead of asking for help, I went back to the old patterns that have done me such a disservice all my life.

Asking for Help

Do you find it hard to ask for help? Does it feel like a sign of weakness? Here are some questions to ask yourself to look behind your feelings about asking for help:

1. True False   When I was growing up, I saw my parents ask for help when they needed it.

2. True False   When I was growing up, other people asked my parents for help.

3. True False   I've always been able to ask my parents for help and know they'd be there for me.

4. True False   In school, I felt comfortable asking my teachers for help as soon as I didn't understand something, even in front of other students.

5. True False   In school, I only asked my teachers for help privately.

6. True False   In school, I never asked my teachers for help.

7. True False   In school, I thought the kids who asked for help were stupid.

8. True False I've had at least one mentor in my life I could turn to for help.

9. True False I seek help in books.

10. True False I seek help at seminars and workshops.

11. True False I seek help via the Internet.

12. True False If I'm in the midst of a crisis that I did not cause, I am okay with asking for help.

13. True False When I get into trouble due to my own mistakes, I feel too ashamed to tell anyone.

14. True False I'm afraid that if key people in my life really knew how messed up I am, they wouldn't like me any more and might even leave me.

15. True False Asking for help feels like admitting that I'm weak.

16. True False I am allergic to feeling vulnerable.

17. True False I don't mind it when others ask me for help.

18. True False I am honored when others feel safe to be vulnerable with me.

19. True False I hate feeling like a bother to anyone, including God.

20. True False I really can't wrap my mind around the idea of God's grace; how can he love me even when I've totally messed up again and again?

21. True False I don't like asking for help because then I feel uncomfortable until I can return the favor.

22. True False I have little tolerance for people who sabotage their own lives by making poor choices.

23. True False Most people don't really need help; they just need more self-discipline.

24. True False I believe the old expression "God helps those who help themselves."

25. True False I love the idea of being a self-made woman.

Why do we let ourselves get to a place of isolation and pain? Here are some reasons why I struggle in this way:

"Asking for help makes me look weak."

"I'm more comfortable as a giver than a taker."

"I don't want to be a bother to anyone else."

"I want to be seen as capable."

Refusing to Ask for Help

Many of us feel that asking for help is a sign of failure—if I can't do it myself, I have no value.

And why would we think any other way? We love the classic loner who is able to rely on their own strength and wits to solve their problems. Think classic comic book heroes, popular nonfiction books with strong female protagonists like *Eat, Pray, Love* and *Wild,* and the cool, outcast loner like Molly Ringwald's character in *Pretty in Pink.* We don't want to rely on anyone else to get us out of our messes. We want to be the heroine of our own stories.

When I start to feel this way, I think of all the ways my husband and I help each other. I'm more of a starter—I have the energy and excitement to carry new ideas and get other people on board. Roger is the one who can make a plan, stick to it, and actually get the project completed. We need to ask for help—there is almost no task that we are designed to do alone. God has formed us to need partners whether it's your husband, your coworker, or your best friend.

Hesitancy to Say No

When we say yes to someone's request, we are often saying no to something that we should have on our list. If your list is filled with other people's yeses, your life is probably filled with enough noes to make you miserable. People-pleasers are concerned with pleasing everyone but themselves. One of the best ways we can ask for help is help in saying no.

Fear

Control issues are based in fear. When you can't let go of the details, when you can't trust others with what God has called them to, you are letting fear control your list—and your life.

Why do we do this to ourselves?

One Rebel's Story

There was this guy, you know the type. Tall, fit, tan, the kind of guy who wore his sunglasses at night. He was exciting. He was also unemployed, living with his mother and really, really messed up. Thing is, I really adored his mom. One weekend, I invited him to go to a friend's house with me, you know, to keep him out of trouble, as a favor.

He was one of the funniest people I had ever met. Clearly, he needed saving. I was just the girl to do it.

I told him he could hang around, you know, watch my place while I was gone. It wasn't long before I was supporting both of us. When I realized most of the jokes were recycled movie lines and unemployment *was* his job, I considered escape. His timely proposal changed my mind. We were engaged.

I promised I would marry him. Everyone said I would be so good for him. He was getting his life together.

My parents hated the idea of my engagement. To leave would be to admit they were right about him.

I got myself into this mess and I would get myself out…

On our wedding day, I drove by myself to face a man so hungover he would fall asleep a few hours later. I daydreamed about turning the car around. Instead, I turned into the driveway. I put on the face of a bride and I kept my promise.

Life got so bad I prayed for death, whether his or mine was irrelevant. The day he left was one of the best days of my life.

My family told me later they would have done anything to spare me that life. If only I had asked.

M. Fletcher

God's Guidance with Help

One of the craziest parts of this whole blame game is how I tend to go to God last when I've really blown it. Just like my sponsor in OA, I want to fix things before I talk to God.

Do I know logically that this is crazy? Yes.

Is it still how I behave? Yes.

That's why this devotion from *Jesus Calling* by Sarah Young hit me so hard when I read it:

> "I do not despise your weakness, My child. Actually, it draws Me closer to you, because weakness stirs up My compassion—My yearning to help...I have gifted you with fragility, providing opportunities for your spirit to blossom in My presence...Rather than struggling to disguise or deny your weakness, allow Me to bless you richly through it."[24]

God wants to richly bless me through my weakness, as even the apostle Paul discovered:

> And finally He said to me, "My grace is enough to cover and sustain you. My power is made perfect in weakness." So ask me about my thorn, inquire about my weaknesses, and I will gladly go on and on—I would rather stake my claim in these and have the power of the Anointed One at home within me. I am at peace and even take pleasure in any weaknesses, insults, hardships, persecutions, and afflictions for the sake of the Anointed because when I am at my weakest, He makes me strong (2 Corinthians 12:9-10, The Voice).

I've been a speaker and writer of some form or another for most of my adult life. When I first started out in my early twenties, I would choose to write and talk about subjects that I felt I'd mastered. Freezer cooking and entertaining on a budget were my go-to topics. I would speak and write and people would ooh and ahh because I would give them ideas and inspiration.

Because I wanted to grow in my speaking and writing skills, I looked to those I admired: Liz Curtis Higgs and Marilyn Meberg were two of my favorites. As I studied the way they delivered their messages, one thing became abundantly clear: they talked more about their failures than they did about their accomplishments.

Their stories, some heartbreaking, most hilarious, were raw and honest and the ones I most identified with. It was the first time I had an inkling that people could learn more from my mistakes than they ever could from my thinking I had an area of my life "together."

So I started speaking more from my brokenness than from my victory. And that's when people started to relate to my magazine articles and presentations more than ever before. There is something powerful in the message that we are not alone in our pain and our mistakes, but that with the help of others, and a grace-filled God, we can see recovery and healing.

Rebels Ask for Help

When I was a young mom, I was heavily involved in volunteering at our new church, Bay Horizons. It was a startup church and there was no lack of roles that needed to be filled and things that needed to be done. The person in charge of community was our pastor's wife, Kim. Not only did Kim have a full-time job, but it was up to her to see that about 50 percent of what was supposed to happen on Sunday mornings and Wednesday nights happened.

Kim kept acquiring new roles and responsibilities at church, but she had a system for dealing with this: every new job that would come along, Kim would take it on, figure out how to do it with excellence, train someone else to do it, and then turn it over to them.

Each and every time, Kim asked for help. People weren't offended that she asked, they wanted to help. Not only did Kim help get a ministry off the ground, she trained dozens of leaders who went on to serve and lead in churches around the world.

When we refuse to ask for help, especially when it's a mess we've helped create, we resort to two powerful tools: *shame* and *blame*.

Shame comes when our value is found in what we accomplish, not who we are or who created us. When we fail to perform in the way we think we should, shame bubbles to the top.

To be the rebels we are designed to be, we need to look at failure as a very possible outcome. It's not something to be avoided; it's something to be recovered from quickly, learned from, and then built on.

Rebels live risky lives. Failure is always an option.

One year at a conference I attended at Willow Creek Church in Illinois, churches were invited to nominate their own biggest failures.

Willow Creek was saying by this that you can't succeed big if you're not willing to fail big.

Blame makes us feel better in the moment. "If only the committee had given me more time…" "If only my kid hadn't been sick last night…" It feels good to have a reason why things didn't go according to plan. And sometimes there *are* reasons why our plans fell through. But I know that I can run out of gas and instantly think of several reasons it wasn't my fault:

- My daughter didn't fill up the tank.
- I wasn't the last one to drive it.
- I was running late because Roger couldn't find his keys and I didn't notice the gas gauge.
- I wasn't feeling well because the cat kept me up all last night.

Now let me be clear: *blame has nothing to do with accountability.* If I'd asked my daughter to fill up the tank and she didn't, then I need to hold her accountable for that. But if I said, "Sure, you can use my car," and then expected her to fill up my tank without asking, well, that's more than most twenty-year-olds are going to do.

What Braver Living Looks Like

So how do we practice being brave when it comes to asking for help?

Realize you are probably helping others all the time. Brené Brown says that when we refuse to ask others for help, we are secretly judging those we help. People want to feel helpful, and when we, the self-sufficient women we are, ask others for help, it helps them to know that we value them and that we respect who they are.

Model asking for help. I know you are strong and capable—that's why I need to see you saying, "I can't do this, I need your help." Going through life never "owing" anyone is a miserable way to live. Be brave—put it out there. That way your friends and kids don't have to pretend they have it all together to keep up with you.

Stop defaulting to blame. Blaming yourself, blaming others—neither is healthy when it's just human error. We all make mistakes. Fail quickly, then get up quickly.

Share your weakness. I love how raw, honest, and totally unfiltered my friend Erin is about her life as a working mom. She writes: "I'm totally and completely failing at life right now. And not just a little bit."[25]

Erin goes on to detail her day of taking her kids to the park only to have her two-year-old's feet covered in splinters, forgetting her wallet before going to the gym with all of her kids in tow, bumming twenty dollars off a friend to get her brood dinner as they run off to basketball practice, only to have that same two-year-old throw up said dinner all over himself and Erin. Then realizing she was nearly out of gas with no wallet and no money. Erin continues:

> We made it home. I have no idea if my car has enough gas to get to the gas station tomorrow, but I'm not thinking about that right now. I have puke-covered clothes to wash and a sobbing toddler who is screaming "I'm hungry" and two exhausted big kids who need to go to bed and...
>
> I'm a mess.
>
> A total mess.
>
> And I haven't even told you about the recent toothpaste incident or Chai tea latte incident or car breaking down incidents (yes, that's plural) or the broken water main or the fact that I totally screwed up a client campaign at work. I haven't shown you pictures of the pile (no, mountain) of unfolded laundry sitting in my room or the piles of dog hair sitting in the corners of my kitchen.[26]

As I continued to read, I realized that I have been Erin. I knew some of what she was going through, but I hadn't sat down and totaled up everything that was crashing down around her. No wonder she was on edge; no wonder she was feeling overwhelmed.

But Erin did something brave. Instead of telling herself it was OK, that she just needed to plow through it, she posted it. She took to the Internet and said here is how I'm failing. And that one act of bravery made all the difference.

Dozens and dozens of women jumped on her blog and took to her

Facebook page, and while Erin was sitting in the mud, feeling like a failure, these women climbed in the mud with her. They said the most powerful words a woman can speak to another woman:

"Me too!"

"I'm so sorry. I've been there. It hurts. It will get better."

"I love you. You are not failing. You are normal."

And that is where the real rebels take up the cause. To rally around a friend and say, "I know. None of us is perfect. I need help all the time. Let's help each other."

Tiny Acts of Rebellion

1. I will ask my husband's/friend's/coworker's advice on a problem even if I feel like I should figure it out on my own.

2. I will say yes when my husband asks, "Can I help with dinner" (even if he really doesn't mean it).

3. I will post a problem on Facebook and ask for help whether it's about cooking, finding the best babysitter, or looking for joy.

4. I will say yes when the bagger at the grocery store asks me if I'd like help out to my car.

5. I will say yes when I'm sick and a friend asks if she can bring me dinner.

Tips for Each Rebel Type

Expressive

When you avoid asking for help, it's often because you're too embarrassed. Your personality tends to get labeled "the airhead" and you don't want your need for help to prove that label true. Much of the time, however, you're more than happy to ask for help. Sometimes you ask sooner than you really need it because you want the company or you want someone else to do the heavy lifting for you. Be careful not to take advantage of helpful friends or you may find them scarce when you're in real trouble.

Analytic

Of all the personalities, you are most mortified by the thought of admitting that you've made a mess. You may even lie to cover up a mess, rationalizing that since it shouldn't have happened it can't have happened, so it's not a lie because it's all so unthinkable. Seeking forgiveness can be excruciating and forgiving yourself all but impossible. Often, you'll try to make up for it rather than apologizing, because that would mean actually admitting to a mistake. The more you receive God's grace, the easier all of this will become.

Driver

You tend to take a pragmatic approach. If you mess up, you seek a quick fix and move on. "It is what it is" is a favorite phrase; you see no need to cry over spilt milk. The danger of your tendency to move right along is that you may ignore actual damage that's been done to key relationships and fail to take the time to repair them. Just because you're over it doesn't mean everyone else is or even should be. The Performancism bully wants nothing more than for you to neglect key relationships, so intentionally care for them instead.

Amiable

You often have no idea how you've gotten yourself into the mess you're in. Often, it's due to your own inactivity or failure to make a choice. Once in the mess, you may think you have to stay there, feeling as if you don't deserve any better or waiting for someone to come rescue you on their own. Learning to advocate for yourself is a vital life skill, and it starts with learning what options are available to you for getting out of the mess. Often asking for help means asking for information too.

CHAPTER 20

No Is a Complete Sentence

Why this two-letter word is the most powerful one in your vocabulary.

❋

"My early attempts at saying no were often far from graceful, but with practice even my no came from a place of love. Love yourself enough to be able to say yes or no."

Susan Gregg

Bully belief 12: "*No* is a dirty word."

My (Cheri's) only task on Career Day was to monitor the students who came in and out of my classroom to hear two presenters. The kids were attentive; the real-estate agent and architect were superb. I was under no stress. In fact, I was *relaxed.*

Suddenly, a student dashed into the room, gasping, "Mrs. G! My mom needs a thumb drive!"

Knowing his mother was a presenter in another room, I reached into my purse, grabbed the first thumb drive I touched, and tossed it across the room to him.

"You're a lifesaver, Mrs. G!" he shouted, rushing out.

The entire exchange took less than ten seconds. But for the next hour, I felt like a hero. Once again, I'd rescued someone's day, in my own small way.

Later that day, I sat down with my laptop to grade my students' English projects. I reached for the three thumb drives I knew were in my purse and froze when I found only two.

Oh yeah, I loaned one. Worry gnawed my stomach. *No, I'm sure odds are in my favor. I still have two of the three thumb drives. The one I need is sure to be here.*

Seconds later, I was reminded why I don't gamble. I had two thumb drives all right, but the projects weren't on either one. I ransacked my purse. Tore apart my desk. Searched the floors. *No third thumb drive.*

I texted my student. He had no idea where mine was. "Sorry, Mrs. G!" *Sorry? That's it? I can't believe…Of all the ungrateful…I didn't even think twice before I…*Wait a minute. *I didn't even think* once.

I reacted out of instinct to solve someone else's problem without evaluating my own needs. And now I'm mad at him? Whose responsibility was it to say no? Or at least "Hang on—let me check to see if there's anything vital on here that I wouldn't want to lose"? Or even "If you can wait five minutes, I can help. If you need one faster, ask someone else"?

Mine, of course. But sometimes I feel like my brain's been programmed to a default "say yes first, ask questions later" setting.

The Rip Current of People-Pleasing

In her *What Happens When Women Say Yes Devotional,* Lysa Ter-Keurst says, "Dead giveaway I'm in the rip current of people pleasing—when I dread saying yes but feel powerless to say no." [27]

I live near a beach on the Monterey Bay where swimming is strictly forbidden due to deadly rip currents. Every year, visitors ignore the "No Swimming" signs, dive into the ocean for a refreshing swim, and get swept out to sea. After they're rescued, they have new reverence for the power of a rip current.

"I'm a strong swimmer, but no matter how hard I tried, it was too much for me!" they say.

People-Pleasing is a rip current. When we ignore the warning signs and dive in, we will be overwhelmed by overcommitment. No matter how strong a personality we have, or how hard we work, People-Pleasing will overpower us every time.

Why? We are not designed to please people. We are designed to please God.

When we try to please people, they'll take all we offer and expect more. As long as we keep on saying yes, they keep on taking. We feel drained, used, even abused. But as long they can count on us to save the day, they'll keep bringing us their emergencies du jour.

We may start thinking *I can't believe they…*and *I never meant for them* *to...*, which leads to bitterness and resentment. But as much as we want to blame others for how victimized we feel, it's ultimately not their fault. We're the ones who saw the sign and dove in anyway.

How far out are you being dragged by the rip current of People-Pleasing? This self-assessment will help you determine the strength of its pull on you:

1. When others ask me for help, I feel
   a) flattered.
   b) curious.

2. When I'm asked to be involved in a project, I
   a) feel needed.
   b) assess my motives.

3. I say yes
   a) because I'm afraid to say no.
   b) only when I mean that I can commit fully from start to finish.

4. When commitments outside the home take priority over my family,
   a) I expect them to understand and roll with it.
   b) I reassess my commitments and priorities.

5. Disappointing other people
   a) terrifies me.
   b) happens every day.

6. When I disappoint someone,
   a) I feel like a failure.
   b) her disappointment is her issue to deal with.

7. Intellectually, I know it's not possible for everyone to like me,
   a) but I keep trying.
   b) and this reality guides my yes and no choices.

8. When someone asks me to make an immediate decision,
   a) I often cave into the pressure and just say yes.
   b) my answer is usually no.

9. If I don't have my calendar with me,

    a)   I tend to say yes and hope it doesn't conflict with anything.

    b)   I say, "I'll get back to you after checking my preexisting commitments."

10. If my spouse or children aren't with me,

    a)   I often say yes and then may or may not remember to tell them about my new commitment.

    b)   I wait until I can confer with them to make a new commitment.

11. When I hear, "If you don't do it, it won't get done,"

    a)   I say yes because I'm their last hope.

    b)   I say, "Well, if nobody feels called to do it, perhaps it isn't going to happen this year."

12. Once I've said yes,

    a)   I find a way to back out if I didn't really mean it.

    b)   I stick to my commitment.

13. Once I understand all the details,

    a)   I realize that I shouldn't have committed without asking questions.

    b)   I am in a position to give a thoughtful yes or no.

14. I say yes

    a)   to my idea of what the other person is asking me.

    b)   after I've learned what the other person has in mind.

15. I say yes

    a)   to many commitments that require me to do things I'm not good at.

    b)   only to requests that tap into my strengths and spiritual gifts.

16. When someone lays on enough guilt,

    a)   I'll say yes to almost anything.

    b)   I am likely to say no because I don't want to work with someone who relies on such unhealthy manipulative tactics.

The more *a* answers you gave, the greater pull People-Pleasing has on your life.

Why We Must Stop Being "Somebody" and "Anybody"

An uncomfortable silence hung in the room. We all avoided eye contact. Our leader repeated the question: "We need *Somebody* for this project. Can *Anybody* volunteer?"

I sighed a very old sigh. It's one I'd been sighing for more than three decades. As far back as my teens, I'd answered to these two names: *Somebody* and *Anybody*.

When *Nobody Else* volunteered, *Everyone* could count on me to finally raise my hand. After all, I could do the task. I was capable. Qualified. Gifted, even. And as *Everyone* knows, "With great gifts come great responsibilities." Besides, it wasn't that hard: *Anybody* could do it!

Looking back, I'm still stunned that it's taken me so many decades to realize that

- my name is neither *Somebody* nor *Anybody*.

- I am not some generic interchangeable part in the giant machine of life.

- while I was off doing things that *Anybody* could have done, my children relied on *Nobody* to be their mother.

- my husband frequently turned to *Nobody* to be his wife.

The belief that "*Somebody—Anybody!*—has to do it" held me captive for far too long.

Have you ever answered to *Somebody* and *Anybody* more quickly than to your own name? If so, here are three reasons on my growing list of why I've stopped answering to *Somebody* and *Anybody*:

1. I end up doing things that might be better left undone.

"*Somebody* has to do it" is not always true. Often, this phrase is followed by some variation of "we've always done it," which does not mean it still needs to be done. Some plans need to fail. Some traditions need to die. Some organizations need to discover through lack of team buy-in that they're on the wrong track.

When *Somebody* and *Anybody* stepped in at the last minute, I often prevented much-needed change and learning from occurring.

2. The best person for the task is not always me.

Just because I can do something does not mean I should. Just because the pressure is on doesn't mean I have to cave and say, "OK! OK! I can't handle the guilt trip!"

Sometimes, other people are waiting to see if the Rescuers—good old *Somebody* and *Anybody*—are going to swoop in and save the day again. When I did, I often deprived others of opportunities to stretch out of their comfort zones and play integral parts on the team.

3. I neglect my true identities and highest callings.

More than twenty-five years ago, I made a vow before God to be Daniel's *Only Wife*. I'm Annemarie's and Jonathon's *Only Mother*. To my students, I'm their *Only Mrs. G*. And I'm the *Only Me* that God made.

These are my highest callings and truest identities. While I have others, these are my top priorities. For too many years, I poured my prime time and energy into my *Somebody* and *Anybody* roles. *Only Wife, Only Mother, Only Mrs. G,* and *Only Me* got whatever was left over—which wasn't much.

God's Perspective on No

Jesus said that wise women say no.

I was stunned to discover this. It's in the parable of the ten virgins who were waiting for the bridegroom to arrive. The five women who took extra oil for their lamps were called "wise" while the five who didn't remember extra oil were labeled "foolish." The messages I've heard drawn from this story have been about preparation.

Never once have I heard a sermon preached from Matthew 25:1-13 highlight that Jesus told a story in which women who said no were called wise. When the foolish virgins asked the wise virgins to share their oil, the wise virgins said, "No, there may not be enough for both us and you. Instead, go to those who sell oil and buy some for yourselves" (Matthew 25:9).

I notice four things in this passage:

1. When the wise women were asked by the foolish to share their readiness resources, the wise said no.

2. The wise women recognized that if they shared, the result could be everyone "burning out."

3. The wise women were unwilling to suffer the consequences of the foolish failing to prepare.

4. The wise women instructed the foolish to solve the problem caused by their own neglect.

Since realizing that Jesus said wise women say no, I've been asking myself these questions:

- What is my oil? What resources do I need to wisely keep fully stocked?

- When I give from these reserves, who benefits? Who suffers? Who learns?

I pray to discern a foolish no from a wise no. There is a difference between selfishly hoarding what God has given me to share and protecting what keeps me in relationship with him.

How to Say an Intentional Yes

When saying yes, it's vital to be clear what you're saying yes to. Have you ever said yes to a general idea, only to wish you'd said no when the details emerged?

Me too. Not pretty.

In his book *Stumbling on Happiness*, Daniel Gilbert explains why we do this. When we see blurry little black specks on a prairie horizon, for example, we realize they are buffalo far away. We don't look at them and think, "They are tiny; thus, they must be insects." The fact that they are vague and small signals to our brains that they're far away.[28]

On the flip side, we recognize actual insects not only because they are small but also because we see their wings and legs; we see details. Visually, we recognize that vagueness and blurriness indicate distance while details signal closeness.

However, when we deal with time, things get complicated. When you see something on the horizon of your future, it's vague and blurry.

You have a feel for it, which is typically the "why" of the future event. Often, you make your decisions based on this why factor.

But as that vague and blurry future gets closer, becoming the up-close detailed present, you can feel shocked by all the details. The myriad details of the "how" may make you feel, "I never agreed to all this!"

For example, if two months ago you said, "Yes, I'd love to volunteer for the PTO," you were probably excited by the concept of helping out at your child's school. But when the time actually arrived and the details became clearer, the reality of tons of meetings, emails, and paperwork bore no resemblance to why you initially agreed to this task.

When you say yes only to the *why of a concept*, you're going to be blind-sided by the *how of the details*. To help you say an integrated yes—one that includes the *why* and the *how*—try these three steps prior to saying yes:

1. Ask for time to think. Set aside time for quiet contemplation and prayer. Then set a timer for thirty minutes and brainstorm the details that need to be handled in order for this commitment to be successful.

2. Take your list to a significant other, preferably someone of an opposite personality, and ask what worst-case scenarios you've left off your list. Invite them to rain on your parade. After all, precommitment is when you want (or at least need) to have your spirits dampened.

3. Prayerfully consider whether you can say yes to everything on the list, not just the vague and blurry why of glory, but to all the nitty-gritty details required.

Then, if you say no, thank heaven for all involved.

If you say yes, take those brainstormed details, prioritize them, and then write them throughout your calendar. Chipping away at them a little bit at a time will remind you that you've given an integrated yes to the entire commitment.

How to Give the Gift of a Gracious No

These eight steps can help you find freedom to say no, even in the most seemingly desperate situations:

Pray for Discernment

If you hear God calling you to contribute, the rest of these steps are irrelevant. When God asks you to get involved, trust and obey. However, if you skip this vital first step, you may mistake your own compulsion to seek control for conviction.

Pause. Pray. Be still and know that it's God calling before answering yes.

Recognize the Risk of Escapism

Saying yes to a new project can feel like a great way to get out of old commitments that have lost their original luster. This, of course, becomes a never-ending cycle of escaping one old-and-boring project by diving into a momentarily new task, which will soon feel just as old-and-boring as the abandoned one.

Pause. Pray. Honor prior commitments before taking on new ones.

Ask for Full Details

How many times have you said yes to a small task, only to discover it was merely the tip of an iceberg? Brainstorm detailed questions about exactly *what* will be expected of you, *when*, for *how long*, and *what* help and resources will be available. Ask now so you won't be blindsided with unspoken expectations later.

Pause. Pray. Withhold your yes until you know what *they* think it means.

Analyze the Time and Energy Required

You've probably committed to tasks you technically had the time for. But what about energy? Look to see what energy drainers were already scheduled before and after this new event. Intentionally schedule time to refuel before, during, and after. You've been trained to focus so much on time management that perhaps you neglect your greater need: energy management.

Pause. Pray. Know what gives you energy and what drains you; factor this into your final say.

Warning: When you start paying attention to your personal energy management needs, you may feel the sudden urge to compare yourself to other women who seem to do it all and make it look effortless. You may feel compelled to say yes as a way to prove that you have what it takes. More than ever: Pause. Pray.

Ponder Who Will Define Success (and How)

Think through these two scenarios:

What if your standards for success end up being higher than those you say yes to? Will you quit because you don't want to be associated with a low-quality project? Will you take over and finish it "the way it should be done"?

Or what if your standards for success are higher than necessary for the task, but you just can't let go? How will you handle being told, "That's enough. We're done. Let's move on"?

Pause. Pray. Figure out your minimum standard for success before saying yes.

Reflect Realistically on Past Pain

Oh, it wasn't that bad.

Go back and reread your journal excerpts. You know, the ones that start, "I am so overwhelmed. I can't wait until this is over!" Your emails to friends that say, "I'm going insane!" and "Why do I always do this to myself?"

Ask those who live with you.

Pause. Pray. Recognize that *oh, it wasn't that bad* is a distortion of the truth. So is *this time will be different.*

Invite Input from Stakeholders

Ask those to whom you are *Only Wife. Only Mother. Only Best Friend. Only Daughter. Only Sister. Only Aunt.* Ask them to be honest. Otherwise, those who love us may tell us what they think we want to hear because they believe that's what love requires.

But love does not lie. Love tells the truth…

- ahead of time
- before there's an empty seat at the table or soccer game
- prior to resentment becoming bitterness

Pause. Pray. Ask for honest input from those who are your original commitments, your highest priorities.

Ask, "Do They Need Me or Just Somebody/Anybody?"

God will often ask you to step out of your comfort zone. He has all sorts of unexpected ways of helping you grow and become who he created you to be. But if you feel your true self shrinking with each yes, something's wrong. If who you are dies a little bit with each task, chances are you're spending so much time as *Somebody* or *Anybody* that you're losing your self.

No, I'm not suggesting that you become selfish. And no, I don't know where the line between selflessness and loss-of-self lies for you. But the Holy Spirit does.

Pause. Pray. Each yes to God will make you more your true self, not less.

One Rebel's Story

Writer and friend Christi McGuire shares this story of making a seemingly small but incredibly brave choice.

> I had actually resisted automatically saying yes just to say yes. As much as I wanted to put a check in the box of "I want to be a Room Mom," I didn't. I was proud of myself!
>
> But then a second note came home that I couldn't ignore: "No one has volunteered; please consider being this year's Room Mom for your child's kindergarten class."
>
> I had to say yes. What if no one else did? What if the sweet five-year-olds never got a class party or holiday crafts or extra goodies because I said no. I never say no. I *can't* say no!
>
> My daughter's blue eyes pierced my soul: "Pleeeease, Mommy?"
>
> I held the note in my hand, eyes glued to it for a long time.
>
> *I…I…I just can't,* I finally said to myself.
>
> I told my daughter that I wanted to enjoy her class parties with her, not be in charge and make sure everybody *else* was having a good time. Plus, Pinterest-perfect food trays, party décor, and holiday crafts are not where my gifts and talents are. I hung my head in shame, avoiding any eye contact with the teacher next time I was at school.

At the first class party, I timidly stepped in the room. I was more than pleasantly surprised. I was in awe! Not only had someone else stepped up to the position, but she *was* the most wonderful, perfect Room Mom the class could ever have.

If I had said yes instead of no, I would have deprived someone else of using her talents and receiving joy and accolades. And I would have deprived myself of truly being who I am.

Maybe saying no to some things will make it easier to say yes to the right things.

Exactly. As you stop saying yes when you want to say no, you'll start living braver. And when you say no to detractors, you can say yes to what really matters most. When you give the gifts of an intentional yes and a gracious no, fear loses and love wins.

Tiny Acts of Rebellion

1. I will practice saying no in a polite, pleasant tone of voice until it becomes comfortable and natural.

2. I will give my family permission to let me know when they hear me saying yes to everyone but them.

3. When someone says a necessary no to me, I will thank her for her honesty.

4. I will learn about the spiritual gifts God has given me and pray for guidance about when to use them.

5. I will look for other ways to be supportive when I give a necessary no.

Tips for Each Rebel Type

Expressive

Of all the personality types, you're the most likely to say an enthusiastic *yes!* because you love being included and starting new projects.

Details, however, are not your strong suit. If you don't find out what a new commitment involves ahead of time, you may find yourself saddled with a lot of dull, behind-the-scenes work you never would have agreed to. When you're tempted to make an excuse and back out, stick with it and use this memory to help you say no to too many details next time.

Analytic

You know you're the only person around who gets things done to a high standard of excellence. You often say yes to requests because you see yourself as someone who improves the world one detail at a time. Often, those who live with you fail to appreciate your attention to detail, so you find it gratifying when others not only recognize but actually welcome your skills. Don't let your drive to perfect the world, and the recognition you get while doing so, take you away from living with and loving your imperfect family.

Driver

You know that you can accomplish two to three times as much as the average person. So it just makes sense that if something needs to be done, you should step up to the plate. Be sure to build in margins. If you get too many plates spinning and then have an emergency, everything will crash. Manage your energy. If you don't take continual care of your physical needs, your "get up and go" is going to "get up and leave."

Amiable

You hate disappointing people, so you often say an immediate yes to produce a smile rather than a frown. However, sometimes you mean, "Yes, I'll consider your request," when the requester hears, "Yes, I'm committing to do this." Take the initiative to clarify in the moment rather than allow assumptions to grow. Other times, you're tempted to say yes and then just not show up when the time comes. Don't. Say your no with words. Keep your reputation as someone others can count on strong.

Final Encouragements for Living Braver

✳

Dear Reader,

We are so grateful that you've made this journey with us. We know how much it takes to make big (or little changes) in your life. Just a few final encouragements for you:

- Pick One Thing. Find the chapter of this book that hit you square between the eyes and start there. Find one tiny act of rebellion and make it happen, whether it's saying no to bringing snacks for the tenth time in a row to your book club or taking an hour to rest without feeling guilty about the undone dishes.

- Find a Bravery Buddy. Doing anything new and unfamiliar takes courage, and you double your courage when you are being brave together. Between your 40 percent brave and your friend's 40 percent brave, you're at 80 percent brave. And that's enough.

- Practice Empathy. As you start to live braver, you will start to recognize other women around you doing so in their own small ways. Let's all make this world a safer place for women who are stepping out on wobbly legs to be countercultural and live braver.

- Share Your Story. When you tell others what you've done to start living braver, you give women the courage to take the next tiny step forward in their own lives. Join us on Facebook at www.Facebook.com/TinyActsOfRebellion and our website www.TheCureForThePerfectLife.com to share your story and encourage another woman.

Cheering you on,
Kathi and Cheri

Acknowledgments

Kathi would like to thank…

Roger, always.

Amanda, Jeremy, Justen, and Kimberly, who were the first cure for the perfect life. Love you.

Our families, the Richersons, the Lipps, and the Dobsons. You look at us and think, "Yeah, that makes sense," while the rest of the world shakes their heads.

My bravery buddies: Susy Flory, Erin MacPherson, Michele Cushatt, Crystal Paine, and Renee Swope. You encourage me to be every crazy thing God created me to be.

And Cheri. You are the Secret Sauce in everything I do. You are the best example I know of someone who has gone from "trying harder to living brave," and you inspire me every single day.

Cheri would like to thank…

Mother, for sharing your love of reading and always wanting the very best for me.

Daddy, for sharing your love of storytelling and always telling me, "I'm so glad you picked me to be your daddy."

John, for teaching me to speak fluent sarcasm and giving me a plethora of great stories to tell.

Annemarie and Jonathon, for cheering me on through my midlife growing pains and putting up with more bad puns than are likely even legal.

Adelle and Shonna, for lavishing soul-sister encouragement when I needed it most.

Clifford and Dixie, for providing a safe space to find my voice and helping me discover the power of caring feedback.

Amy Carroll, for coaching me to drill down to the core of each message and being as excited as I was each time I finally found it.

Kathi, for sharing the quote that made a rebel out of me ("To avoid criticism, say nothing, do nothing, be nothing") and for being the best Bravery Buddy ever.

Daniel, for believing in me no matter what and making my spiritual growth your number one priority.

Jesus, for rescuing me and delighting in me.

"One Rebel's Story" Contributors

To the amazing women who shared their authentic experiences for all of us to learn from: our admiration, our thanks, and our promise of a trip to Starbucks the next time we see you!

Lindsey Bell is the author of *Searching for Sanity: 52 Insights from the Parents of the Bible*. She's also a minister's wife and stay-at-home mother of two boys. She blogs weekly about faith and family at www.lindsey -bell.com.

Lisa Bogart writes, knits, and hikes in the San Francisco Bay area. She works part-time in a knit shop. Lisa is loving her empty nest, and she and hubby travel more now. You can find her online and check out her monthly giveaway at LisaBogart.com.

Maryleigh Bucher is a wife of thirty years, a mom of five sons ranging in ages from twenty-seven to thirteen. She blogs about the faith, love, and politics of raising boys to men, with grace and joy through the journey, at bluecottonmemory.wordpress.com.

Adelle Gabrielson is wife, boy-mom, writer, and speaker and loves helping other women find their inner shine. With personal stories, humor, and honesty, Adelle shares how to find freedom in our flaws and celebrate our imperfections. Find her personal illuminations on her blog at www.Adel leGabrielson.com.

Sarah Lowther Hensley is a former public radio journalist and college administrator from the beautiful hills of West Virginia. She blogs about her slice of life and her glass-half-full search for good at http:// homeamongthehills.wordpress.com/.

Michelle S. Lazurek is a pastor's wife, a mother, an author, and a speaker. She is a contributing writer for *Movieguide* magazine and a community group leader for Incourage. Visit her website at www.michelle lazurek.com.

Shauna Letellier is married to Kurt and together they have the wild and hilarious privilege of raising three boys who are the catalysts to curing the "perfect" life. She blogs at permissiontobereal.blogspot.com.

Christi McGuire has been in the Christian publishing industry for fifteen years. As an editor and consultant, she enjoys encouraging other writers through the publishing process. She is married to her high-school sweetheart, has two daughters, and loves living by the beaches of the Gulf Coast in Florida. Connect with her at www.ChristiMcGuire.com.

Angela Parlin lives in North Carolina with her husband and four young kids. She blogs about grace and motherhood at www.AngelaParlin.com and would love to have you stop by.

Andé Brescia-Peña shares a life with her husband, their two children, and a vibrant circle of family and friends. She works with teens and young adults, advocating for justice, education, and family stabilization. Connect with her at www.AndePena.com.

Stephanie Shott is an author, international speaker, and founder of The M.O.M. Initiative, a ministry devoted to helping the body of Christ make mentoring missional. To find out more about Stephanie and learn how you can begin a M.O.M. Group in your community and change the world one mom at a time, visit www.themominitiative.com.

Michele Simmons is slightly self-centered, lost in the fray, lovin' every mad, exhausting minute, and trying to grow up to be a servant-hearted Christian. Join her at TravelerInMyOwnBackyard.blogspot.com.

Jenny Lee Sulpizio is a wife and mother of three. She loves to instruct, motivate, and guide other moms with practical advice, tips, and a whole lot of comic relief in the process. Jenny is the author of the recently released guide for all mamas, *Confessions of a Wonder Woman Wannabe.* Find out more about Jenny at www.jennyleesulpizio.com.

Notes

Part 1: Why Trying Harder Only Makes Things Worse

1. Julie K. Gilles, *Prayers for a Woman's Soul* (Eugene, OR: Harvest House, 2013), 230.

2. Bill Gaultiere, "Bible Verses on Perfectionism," *Soul Shepherding* (blog), July 23, 2003, www.soulshepherding.org/2003/07/bible-verses-on-perfectionism.

3. Brené Brown, *The Gifts of Imperfection* (Center City, MN: Hazelden, 2010).

4. www.recreateconference.org/ken-davis-signs-of-life/.

5. Lysa TerKeurst, *What Happens When Women Say Yes to God* (Eugene, OR: Harvest House, 2007), 113.

6. Georgia Shaffer, *Taking Out Your Emotional Trash* (Eugene, OR: Harvest House, 2010), 171.

7. Deborah Smith Pegues, *30 Days to Taming Your Emotions* (Eugene, OR: Harvest House, 2012), 193.

8. Phil Vischer, *Me, Myself, and Bob* (Nashville, TN: Thomas Nelson, 2008), 237.

9. Mary DeMuth, *Beautiful Battle* (Eugene, OR: Harvest House, 2012), 160.

10. Brené Brown, *Daring Greatly* (New York: Penguin, 2013).

11. Donna Jones, "Women Alive! Conference," Fremont, CA, November 2013.

12. Leo Babauta, "The Little Book of Procrastination Remedies," November 4, 2010, *Zen Habits* (blog), http://zenhabits.net/procrastination/.

13. Steven Pressfield. *The War of Art: Break Through the Blocks and Win Your Inner Creative Battles* (New York: Black Irish Entertainment, 2012), 22.

Part 2: How to Trade Try-Harder Living for Braver Living

1. For more in-depth exploration of the personality paradigm, we highly recommend *How to Deal with Annoying People* by Bob Phillips and Kimberly Alyn (Harvest House, 2011). And if you'd like a personality assessment geared specifically for kids, you'll find one in our book *21 Ways to Connect with Your Kids* (Harvest House, 2012).

Part 3: 12 Cures for the "Perfect" Life

1. If you don't recognize this iconic cultural reference, search YouTube for "Fonzie Wrong." You'll thank us.

2. Po Bronson and Ashley Merryman, *NurtureShock* (New York: Twelve, 2009), 22.

3. Daniel Coyle, "The Social Power of Sharing Mistakes," *The Talent Code* (blog), May 3, 2012, http://thetalentcode.com/2012/05/03/the-social-power-of-sharing-mistakes.

4. W. Clarence Schilt and Stephen Schilt, *A Life to Die For* (Nampa, ID: Pacific Press, 2009).

5. Sheryl Sandberg, *Lean In: Women, Work and the Will to Lead* (New York: Knopf, 2013).

6. www.ted.com.

7. Herb Boyd, *Autobiography of a People: Three Centuries of African American History Told by Those Who Lived It* (New York: Anchor Books, 2000).

8. Katie Moisse, "NFL Coaching Culture Boosts Heart Risk," ABC News, November 4, 2013, http://abcnews.go.com/Health/nfl-coaching-culture-boosts-heart-risk/story?id=20776373.

9. Camille Noe Pagan, "What Kind of Angry Are You?" *Prevention*, March 2012, www.prevention.com/mind-body/emotional-health/how-do-you-express-anger.

10. A Complaint Free World, www.acomplaintfreeworld.org.

11. Stephen R. Covey, *First Things First* (New York: Free Press, 1996).

12. *Freaky Friday*, Walt Disney Pictures, 2003.

13. Tony Schwartz, *Be Excellent at Anything* (New York: Free Press, 2011).

14. Tracie Miles, *Stressed-Less Living* (Abilene, TX: Leafwood Publishers, 2012), 159-60.

15. Lissa Rankin, MD, "Are You Addicted to Busyness?," *Passionate Prescriptions for Living and Loving Fearlessly* (blog), December 5, 2013, http://lissarankin.com/are-you-addicted-to-busyness.

16. *Monsters University*, Walt Disney Pictures, 2013.

17. Sandi Brewer, "The Monkey Jar," *Finally Writing* (blog), August 14, 2013, http://sandisings.blogspot.com/2013/08/the-monkey-jar.html.

18. Donald Miller, *A Million Miles in a Thousand Years* (Nashville, TN: Thomas Nelson, 2011).

19. Jaroldeen Asplund Edwards, *The Daffodil Principle* (Salt Lake City, UT: Shadow Mountain, 2004).

20. Kathi Lipp, *The Get Yourself Organized Project* (Eugene, OR: Harvest House, 2012).

21. Sarah Young, "August 29," *Jesus Calling: A 365-Day Journaling Devotional* (Nashville, TN: Thomas Nelson, 2010).

22. James Surowiecki, "Later," *New Yorker*, October 11, 2010, www.newyorker.com/arts/critics/books/2010/10/11/101011crbo_books_surowiecki?currentPage=all.

23. Kathi Lipp, *The Get Yourself Organized Project* (Eugene, OR: Harvest House, 2012), 19-21.

24. Young, "August 12," *Jesus Calling*.

25. Erin MacPherson, "Failing at Life," *Christian Mama's Guide* (blog), January 16, 2014, www.christianmamasguide.com/2014/01/16/failing-at-life/.

26. Ibid.

27. TerKeurst, *What Happens When Women Say Yes to God Devotional* (Eugene, OR: Harvest House, 2013), 112.

28. Daniel Gilbert, *Stumbling on Happiness* (New York: Vintage Books, 2007).

About the Authors

Kathi Lipp is the author of *The Husband Project, The Get Yourself Organized Project, 21 Ways to Connect with Your Kids*, and several other books. Kathi's articles have appeared in dozens of magazines, and she is a frequent guest on Focus on the Family radio and TV. She and her husband, Roger, live in California and are parents of four young adults. Kathi shares her story at retreats, conferences, and women's events across the United States. Connect with her at www.KathiLipp .com, on Facebook at www.Facebook.com/AuthorKathiLipp, or on Twitter @KathiLipp.

Cheri Gregory is a certified personality trainer, contributor to multiple books, including *Wired That Way* and *21 Ways to Connect with Your Kids*, and frequent speaker for MOPS groups, women's retreats, parent workshops, and educational conferences. She is also a high school English teacher and graduate student. Cheri has been "wife of my youth" to Daniel (her opposite personality), a pastor, for over a quarter of a century; they have two college-age kids (who are also opposite personalities). She blogs about expectations, "baditude," and hope at www.CheriGregory.com. Connect with her on Facebook at www .Facebook.com/Cheri.Gregory.Author and Twitter @CheriGregory.

❈

Visit *The Cure for the "Perfect" Life* website
www.TheCureForThePerfectLife.com
and Facebook page
www.Facebook.com/TinyActsOfRebellion

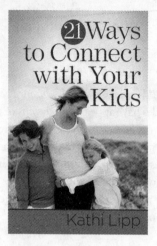

21 Ways to Connect with Your Kids

Parents spend a good chunk of time making sure their kids are okay—they're getting good grades, doing their chores, and just enough cleaning that their rooms won't be condemned if the Board of Health happens to drop by. *21 Ways to Connect with Your Kids* offers a straightforward, workable plan that coaches you to do one simple thing each day for three weeks to connect with your kids.

Daily connection ideas include:

- planning a family fun night
- telling your child what you like about them
- developing a character growth chart
- writing a love note to your child
- working together on a family project

Written in Kathi's warm and personable but thought-provoking tone, this book will motivate you to incorporate great relationship habits into your daily life and give you confidence that you can connect with your kids even in the midst of busy schedules.